GREAT LEGENDS OF WALES

GREAT LEGENDS
OF
WALES

Ronald Barnes

COLIN SMYTHE
Gerrards Cross, 1991

First published in 1991 by Colin Smythe Limited,
Gerrards Cross, Buckinghamshire

British Library Cataloguing in Publication Data

Barnes, Ronald
  Great legends of Wales.
  1. Welsh tales and legends
  I. Title
  398.209429

ISBN 0–86140–317–7

Produced in Great Britain
and printed and bound by Billing & Sons Limited, Worcester

CONTENTS

The Devil's Kitchen

PREFACE

THE DEVIL'S KITCHEN

(Twll Du)

Deep in the heart of Snowdonia, beneath an amphitheatre of towering mountains, lies the mysterious Llyn Idwal.

Long, long ago this wild cwm was the sole province of witches who dwelled in a deep cave set beneath the gigantic rock schism separating Y Garn from The Glyders. Once this brittle defect of nature was known as Twll Du (The Black Cavern) but is now more often referred to as The Devil's Kitchen.

The witches who comprised the infamous Coven of Twll Du were of Druidical origin, highly educated and renowned for their sensuous beauty. Because of these attributes it was not difficult for them to form liaisons with men of power by whom they sometimes bore children, thereby increasing their influence which grew to such an alarming degree that it caused dissentions within their own ranks.

And it was this discord which resulted in the eventual destruction of the cave and the entire Coven save for a witch named Mhaira who was ordered by her Master to take up residence in a rude Derbyshire cottage known as The Devil's Elbow.

There she gave birth to at least two daughters thus founding a direct lineage which lasted over 700 years and inaugurating the dreaded Coven of Broomhead Moor.

The fear which their presence generated in the minds of the country folk was unwarranted for, in reality, they made no macabre threats. On the other hand, the power which Mhaira wielded and subsequently used changed the face of Europe for a hundred years and is still influencing our lives today — as these stories will reveal.

As a point of interest there is reason to believe that the English soldiers who saw the witches in Wales coined the word 'bewitched', forming this from the Anglo-Saxon words *be* (thoroughly) and *wicce* (Female witch) which finally evolved as *wiccian* (enchanted). Thus the word 'bewitched' was intended to mean 'thoroughly enchanting' rather than anything sinister. N.B. *wicce* was pronounced 'witch'.

THE HERITAGE OF GWYNEDD

The turbulent history of Wales has left an undying imprint upon its hospitable people and their unique philosophy of life. Until one is able to understand that, the indefinable magic of Gwynedd will remain a mystery.

Every country and culture possesses a vast heritage of Lore and Legend, their origins deeply rooted in events which took place long before history was recorded in writing or, alternatively, as an extension to their classical mythology which was the very basis of their customs and often religions.

The preservation of these epic narratives we owe to countless generations of old men who loved to relate their tales round ancient camp-fires; and to 'free-lance' minstrels, poets, troubadours and bards who not only served as the disseminators of news but also regaled their audiences with their own particular interpretation of past glories.

Those who gathered to listen were very much like people are to-day, becoming just as bored by constant repetition of stories heard all too often; and the professional raconteurs, being aware of the need to rekindle public interest, endeavoured to meet this demand. Unfortunately they were more concerned with their own advancement than the veracity of their anecdotes. Consequently, rather than spend time researching new material they began to enlarge upon the originals, often weaving supernatural webs around their stories or embroidering them with threads of undue magnificence. And the more inventiveness and ingenuity these early 'historians' displayed, the greater was their reward in terms of wealth and fame. So that in the end it is hardly surprising that the original truth was all but obliterated, while minor incidents took on the status of epic deeds.

These distortions were often aggravated by pride and the desire for person aggrandisement. The multitude of princes and the *uchewyr* (notable personages) employed private bards whose duty was not only to entertain their employer and his guests with an endless repertoire of stories, but also to proclaim the virility, bravery and reputation of their masters. Not unlike certain areas within the media today where future employment and financial rewards are entirely dependent upon success, the bards likewise utilized flattery and exaggeration, while blatant misrepresentation of history was prevalent.

There is no place on earth which, for its size, compares with Gwynedd in the richness, scope and invention of its legends. This is contrary to reason since the Welsh, in company with the Romans, appear to be the only societies in existence which did not possess a heritage of mythology upon which to draw as a source of literary inspiration. It is inconceivable that these tales owe their origins to Celtic polytheism since the Druids, who were the Celts' administrators, judges, teachers and religious leaders, despite being literate in Greek, recorded nothing in writing and in passing on their beliefs to postulants solely by word of mouth, resolutely ensured the continuance of an occult 'closed shop'.

Thus, in AD 78, when the Druids of Anglesea were annihilated by the Romans, virtually the whole of their traditional mysticism died with them, so that little is known of their religious philosophy save that it was a cult which accepted many gods, believed in immortality through rebirth and human sacrifice, and wherein rivers, lakes and the oak-tree played important roles.

The Welsh, like the Romans, must have acknowledged the gap in their tradition but whereas the Caesars blatantly adopted and then Latinized Greek mythology before superimposing upon it a system whereby they themselves could be elevated into gods, the Welsh resolved their problem in a typically individual manner.

They had already accepted the Druidical belief in preordination and reincarnation, possibly because the former provided an excuse when things got beyond them, while, optimistically, the latter gave their souls the chance of finding a more prosperous body to inhabit next time round.

Not unlike the early Christians, they were also influenced by the Concept of the Triune, the three manifestations of a single Deity being an example. As far as they were concerned, this combined admirably with the Hellenic Rites of Passage which encompassed the equally triadic events in life — Birth, Marriage and Death. Finally, as the Red Book of Hergest proves, they assimilated the Trojan conviction that man's fate is ordained in the heavens.

Unlike everyone else, the *cymry* showed little interest in supra-mortal Deities: creations of the imagination with six arms, the body of a bull and the head of a lion surmounted by a wreath of writhing snakes was too much for the down-to-earth Welsh and were accorded no place in their embryo 'mythology'. Dragons they were prepared to accept as quasi-normal animals with the odd *afanc* thrown in for good measure but rather than become involved with super-human divinities in nightmarish forms, they preferred to settle for super-men such as giants, magicians and heroes. Even the inhabitants of their Other World were humans endowed with ultra-human abilities rather than cosmic divinities rendered quasi-human by earthly physical desires.

Having established their own more comfortable brand of what should be termed folklore, the Welsh then embellished it with miracles, magic and marvels wrought by superhuman deeds (always executed by Welshmen, of course). From this, *The Mabinogion* came into being, certainly the pinnacle in medieval story-telling but regarded by some as myth and mythology in decline. The simple truth is that never having had a classical mythology, what the Welsh had, they created themselves, a synthesis of other isms upon which they placed their own stamp. So what was it which evolved?

Legends are usually based upon historical, fabulous or romantic origins though often raised to unmerited significance.

Folktales, on the other hand, are normally heroic nationalistic stories handed down by word of mouth over the centuries and, in order to present a powerful testimony, frequently endowed with religious or magical qualities.

Myths and *Mythology* concern themselves with the gods, supernatural forces, immortality and the 'unknown'.

Finally there are stories of which 'Owain Gwynedd's Silver Dagger' is a perfect example. These are founded upon known historical occurrences, people and places, but by virtue of supernatural references have undoubted mythical overtones together with mysticism such as rites and sorcery practised by wizards and Covens of Witches, particularly those of Druid descent. As such, they are a unique mixture of history, myth, magic, folk-lore and legend, and thus can only be properly described as *Wondertales*.

The legends concerning King Arthur are of a different order revealing what some professors have described as a sad deterioration in the art of classical mythology. Despite this, to the medieval Welsh they represented their 'Heroic and Glorious Age' and became the very strength which fortified them during the times of their worst oppressions. More than the church they became the basis of a fervent 'religion', being to the *Cymry* what the Old Testament is to the Jews, with the dream of Arthur's eventual reincarnation matching the Biblical prophecy of Christ's second coming. And it is not idle speculation to hold that the combination of Arthurian Legends and Wondertales were seen by their foes as a

military strength of the first magnitude. This is borne out by fact. . .
The year 1170 was an auspicious one for King Henry II of England.
First, he had rid himself of the troublesome 'Little Brook' (Thomas à
Becket). Then upon the death of his equally obdurate adversary,
Owain Gwynedd, and the internal strife in Gwynedd which the
Prince's death had occasioned, he felt that the Welsh would be too
distracted by their own afflictions to threaten his western borders.
Only they weren't and the troubles gradually intensified.

In 1189, the king decided to resolve the Welsh problem once and
for all time, but before unleashing his army he considered it essential
to nail the legend of Arthur's immortality for ever. Accordingly, he
hatched a plot whereby the monks of Glastonbury Abbey dug a little
to the south of the Lady Chapel and there 'found' the bodies of King
Arthur and his Queen, Guinevere, likewise 'discovering' proof of
their identities. The latter took the form of a lead cross but the
descriptions of the words upon it, as recorded by Ralph of Cog-
geshall (a King's man if there ever was one) and Giraldus Cambresis,
were as wildly conflicting as the varying accounts of the inscriptions
upon Christ's cross contained in the four gospels. And the Welsh
didn't believe a word of it as events proved.

Unfortunately, the sacking of the abbeys and monasteries
by the Vikings, Henry III and Henry VIII, together with similar
depredations enacted by Cromwell, resulted in an untold wealth
of Legends and Wondertales being destroyed, truncated or
dispersed.

Over the centuries some of these have come to light and having
been long buried and so protected from the inconsistencies of frequent repetition, reveal the original narrative without too much
embellishment. Towards the end of the 18th century a small number
resurfaced in Derbyshire when an aged woman named Mhaira, who
claimed to be a witch, passed them on to a Yorkshire yeoman. And
her Wondertales fall precisely into this category.

Despite the seemingly apocalyptic nature of their source, extensive
research has substantiated the basic stories. The only enigma remaining is that if Mhaira was not directly descended from the Coven of
Twll Du, unless she somehow acquired them from the Cistercian
monks of Fountains or Rievaulx Abbeys — which is most unlikely —
how did she obtain historically correct information which had been
lost to civilization for over 600 years?

The question is, however, purely academic for no matter how in-
ventive a mythologist the originator of these Wondertales may or
may not have been, they undoubtedly were in Mhaira's possession.

Castle of the Winds and Glyder Fach

A VOICE FROM ANTIQUITY

My grandfather hailed from the West Riding of Yorkshire. There, tales of witchcraft and hobgoblins, lore and legend abound, and it is the only part of the British Isles where the word 'black' in place-names rivals the use of 'du' or 'ddu' (black) in Gwynedd. In all these matters he was an acknowledged expert: his knowledge was en-cyclopaedic; his memory, prodigious; and his veracity, renowned.

Over the years he regaled me with tales of the Broadacres, these inevitably centering on Soyland Moor — the wildest place in all England where, legend has it, neither Saint nor Satan dared to tread. And of how a young family settled there in 1774, their firstborn destined to become one of the greatest men of his time — Tom Brackenridge, a man they called the most honest alive, and who was my grandfather's grandfather.

On 14 February 1791, one of the church steeple bearings cracked leaving the tenor bell hanging precariously and threatening to demolish half the nave. The nearest source of thin ropes strong enough to secure the enormous weight was Castleton, forty miles distant over the dreaded Broomhead Moor — the witches' winter home. Tom, then only sixteen but 'standing six and a half feet tall and powerfully proportioned to match with waving silver hair and laughing blue eyes' volunteered to fetch the ropes.

Two days later, on the return journey, a great blizzard swept through Derbyshire forcing him to seek shelter at a remote cottage hard by Devil's Elbow. The door was opened by a tiny, bent ruin of a woman who, according to the locals, had lived there longer than the oldest inhabitant's grandfather could recall, and of whom it was said that she was a witch so old and her powers so enfeebled that: 'she could only charge tuppence for castin' a spell an' no more than a groat durin' Lenten time.'

When she saw Tom on the threshold she immediately fumbled within the folds of her wusted garb and, extracting a shiny object from within, flung it at his feet saying:

'Y maer Dagr Owain Gwynedd yn awr wedi dychwllyd i'w ber-chen priodol' ('The Dagger of Owain Gwynedd hath now returned to its rightful owner').

Later that night the old woman recounted her story.

'Legend has it that I have dwelt here for over 600 years. In a way, that is the truth, for only the body hath changed: the spirit within me is the same. It was in 1170 when Mhaira was commanded by her Prince to leave the great Black Coven of Gwynedd and sojourn here until the next rightful owner of the Silver Dagger should appear unto her — a man in the true Celtic image of Owain Gwynedd himself.

'Since then, eighteen generations have passed until I am the last and without child. And eighteen times hath this story been handed down exactly as it happened for we, whose ancestors were the learned Druids of Anglesea, believe that the traits, the so-called instincts, yea, even parts of the memory pass from one generation unto the next, as with the birds, the body being no more than Nature's carrier of man's characteristics.'

With that, for the first time, the Story of Owain Gwynedd's Silver Dagger was told to one who was not a descendant of the Black Coven of Twll Du. 'Take the dagger,' she advised, 'no harm shall come unto him who keeps it in his possession. Moreover, it is ordained that he who wears it in his belt shall be the next Keeper of Lore and Legend regarding which it is my duty to inform thee well. But return soon for I am nigh unto eighty and cannot have long to dwell upon Apollo's planet.'

I was fortunate in having a history tutor who accepted nothing unless it had been researched and verified by leading scholars of impeccable reputation, particularly that which had been handed down by word of mouth over the centuries and thus, in his opinion, was often distorted beyond recognition. As an example, he repeatedly quoted the havoc wrought upon Scottish history and literature when many — who should have known better — unreservedly accepted the spurious claims made by James Macpherson that he had 'discovered and translated' the 3rd century poems attributed to Ossian, the legendary Gaelic bard.

While I did not question my grandfather's veracity, nor that of his grandfather, I had been so effectively imbued with the basic principles of historicity that the unauthenticated acceptance of these stories, in either historical or legendary vein, was out of the question. Likewise, the alleged manner in which Tom came by them and the reappearance of the Silver Dagger was too equivocal for me to swallow. However, the judgement of youth is often confined to pure black and virgin white completely ignoring the infinite varieties of grey which separate the extremities.

War quickly ensued and, in the limited periods of time available to a soldier, there was such an abundance of contemporary stories about which to write that Gwynedd's past was banished from my mind. Then, when peace arrived, the irresistible call of the Swiss and Austrian alps was heeded so that many years elapsed before I returned to Snowdonia.

One day, while climbing in the Glyders, I noticed that the apex of the long, triangular shadow cast by Castell y Gwynt reached the exact spot where the cave homes of the coven once existed. A detailed search of the location eventually revealed the remnants of Mhaira's cave. Instantly, memory's bell rang loud. And it was only then that I realized that my grandfather's ability as a raconteur was such that despite them having lain dormant for over thirty years, Mhaira's tales were still indelibly imprinted upon my mind. Years of research followed.

This has revealed much which leads me to believe that everything happened as she described it — apart from the super-natural influences. Except that there are some who are not so sure about those either. Like one legendary mountaineer who, at eighty-four was still climbing Scafell and Great Gable alone! One day he confided to me that he hated climbing in Gwynedd.

'There's something chilling about those mountains,' he declared, 'especially the Glyders.'

When I suggested that he may have read too many legends con-cerning witches and so forth he utterly refuted the idea. 'Don't believe in them!' he retorted. 'But never again will I ascend the Glyders!'

Others, like my wife and I, still do, clambering over them and even within the confines of Twll Du, utterly fascinated . . . I sometimes ask myself . . . by what?

Any historian worth his salt will admit that much of medieval history is, at the best, ten per cent fact and ninety per cent con-jecture based upon a sound knowledge of the period concerned. The 'spoken word' I have introduced into Mhaira's stories must obviously be conjectural but this form of presentation was con-sidered essential for the portrayal of these Wondertales in a con-temporary form.

Welsh place-names are dramatically descriptive of their historic or legendary origins, e.g. Bwlch y Saethau means 'Pass of the Arrows', so named because it is supposedly the location of Arthur's final battle where 'flights of arrows fell like winter hail'. Thus to those who are not conversant with the Welsh language, much of the magic of Gwynedd is lost.

Now the ancient Celts were not only poets of great distinction but they possessed a remarkable eye for beauty, their 'legends' invariably being rooted in locations which were either idyllic or magnificent and present day place-names are often monuments to these great deeds. In order that the reader may understand them, I have included a glossary of Welsh words and their translations, the latter sometimes being archaic or colloquial rather than semantically academic. The scope has been extended to cover the descriptive names encountered by visitors to Wales, thereby increasing interest, particularly that of the children who love this particular type of romanticism.

MHAIRA'S WONDERTALES

THE LEGEND OF THE TRIPLE SACRIFICE

(THE LEGEND OF MOEL SIABOD)

(A.D. 1070)

During the 8th century, the whole of England and Wales was stricken by seven years of terrible rain and no place suffered more than the Principality of Gwynedd. All the crops rotted in the fields and half the cattle and sheep died from foot-rot leaving the people starving.

The prayers they offered in the churches went unheard and the people began to murmur that God had forsaken them. On hearing this, the Druid priests congregated on the smooth rock summit of Moel Siabod where they erected a great altar from which they exhorted the multitude to pray unto Apollo that he might send the sun to drive away the rain.

All night long they prostrated themselves, pledging their most priceless possessions in return for a sign. At dawn, a shaft of sunlight pierced the leaden clouds bathing the altar in a golden glow. And this they took as an omen that their invocations had been answered.

Now amongst those present were three young virgins born on the same day to a woman named Cigfa, after the wife of Pryderi. And upon their wrists the priests placed clasps of gold set with flashing garnets exquisitely fashioned in a peculiar phallic design to signify that the wearers were married unto a God of the Other World; while around their necks they draped ropes of pearls, symbolic of the Haloes of Hell. Then, as they incanted a wild dithyrambic, the priests lay the maidens upon the altar where they slew them before interring their bodies in a common grave. Following the ceremony, there were seven years of plenty and more people worshipped at the tumulus than entered the churches.

When news of this reached the bishop he showed his disapproval of the Druid's intercession by placing a curse upon Cigfa: that neither her husband nor the husbands of those descended from her would ever cast their eyes upon a son, save he whose son could not sire either a son or a daughter but whose spouse would bring forth a son of God.

Seven generations passed following which Wales came under
constant attacks by Danes and Norsemen. Despite this, the tribal
leaders were more preoccupied with petty internecine strife than in
banding themselves together to oppose the invaders. And none of
these were more troublesome than the Princes of Powys who were
forever making raids upon Gwynedd.

Eventually Rhodri Mawr became Prince of Gwynedd. He was a
man of culture and great learning who not only dreamed of unify-
ing Wales but also of allying himself with King Alfred of England,
a man of equal enlightenment and scholarship, in order to ensure
peace between their troubled nations.

By a combined feat of arms and diplomacy, Rhodri subjugated
Powys and all the tribes of central Wales before making a brilli-
antly conceived marriage to the Princess Deheubarth of South
Wales and thus achieving both his ambitions.

Having thus become *Bretwalda* (High King), Rhodri rewarded
his followers, one of these being a man named Gwythyr, upon
whom he bestowed a *maenol*[1] near Capel Curig. When Gwythyr
arrived in the parish he found that petty jealousies were rife, revealing problems similar to those which once confronted Rhodri.
Accordingly, he resolved to copy his erstwhile leader and by a
series of clever marriages soon controlled four *maenolydd*,[2] thus
making himself the richest and most powerful landholder in the
cantref.[3]

As time went by, Gwythyr's descendants emulated his success so
that when Badrig inherited the family estate it consisted of nine
maenolydd. Within a year he increased this number to ten by marrying Aranrhod, a profoundly religious girl whose family had all
been slain during the merciless advance of Hugh of Avranches'
Norman hordes through Gwynedd.[4]

Although for Badrig, the union was little more than a device to
acquire land, and in Aranrhod's case the means of gaining a well-to-
do protector, they soon found a deep and abiding love together. During the next ten years she bore him six fine daughters and was eagerly
awaiting the birth of another child — which, being the blessed
seventh, must surely be a son — when Badrig fell victim to typhoid.
And while a grieving widow wept by his graveside, once Aranrhod
returned to their *hendre*[5] and removed her widow's weeds, a face
bereft of all human emotion was revealed. With there being no heir to
the lands, Aranrhod immediately enacted the provisions of Howel
Da's Codified Laws and secured possession of the estate, assuming
the mantle of a tribal chieftain and ruling her sept with a rod of iron.

Three months later Aranrhod gave birth to a son naming him

Germanus after the saint who once led the Christian Britons against the pagan Picts and Scots, defeating them at Mold. And that night she vowed to acquire, by fair means or foul, the two further *maenolydd* necessary to increase the estate to the size of a *commote* thereby ranking her son but one step below a Prince. Nor was that all which filled Aranrhod's mind. If that could be achieved, the way was open for a grand-daughter not merely to consort with princes but to marry one, and if it could not be arranged that he was already the Prince of Gwynedd, perhaps she could be married off to the heir to the Principality, whereupon her son would be the rightful Prince. And with him being descended from the noble Badrig, who knows, he could become *Bretwalda*, the High King of All Wales. And with her being no more than twenty-six, she could still be alive to see his enthronement!

As Germanus approached manhood he grew tall and lithe, his eyes shining blue as the heavens above and his locks glistened like burnished gold. Unlike others, he eschewed the fashion of wearing his hair in the manner of a fringe, sweeping it backwards so that it danced like sunlight in the breeze, and with there not being the slightest tuft of down marring the smoothness of his cheeks or jowl, he was the most beauteous of all men in Gwynedd. And the maidens who came from the length and breadth of the land to gaze upon him, swooned at the sight of his countenance, likening him unto a God. Yet he was contemptuous of their charms, preferring the pursuits of learning and poetry.

At last his mother spoke to him saying: 'Two hundred years have passed since the great Rhodri Mawr rewarded thy brave forebear with a *maenol*, since when thy ancestors have increased their tenancies until they now number ten. Since our illustrious Prince Gruffydd ap Cynan is cruelly exiled in Ireland, shouldst thou die without issue, these lands would be escheat to the Earl of Chester, and all who dwell thereon become no better than bondmen to that accursed Norman lackey. This no true son of Gwynedd can permit. Now thou art of an age to take a wife and in so doing both prevent this coming to pass and also increase thy holding until it becomes a *commote* whereat thou shall be ranked as a Lord of Territories and walk one step behind a Prince of the Realm.'

The months passed without Germanus heeding his mother's warning whereupon she took to railing against him constantly. 'Thou art being neglectful of thy heritage', she castigated, 'and encouraging others who whisper that thou art like Narcissus!'

Now Germanus had a foster-brother named Neigwl who had been granted an adjacent *maenol* where he lived with Winifred, his wife of six months standing and who was already with child. Being angered by Aranrhod's incessant tirade and also seeing the great contentment which Winifred had brought to her husband, he considered that he could do much worse than ask for her sister, a beautiful and well-endowed maiden named Gwladys. Thus he sought his sister-in-law's advice as to whether she thought Gwladys would consent to becoming his wife.

And she answered saying: 'When first my sister saw thee, her face coloured the hue of the rising sun and a love for thee filled every part of her body until she now sits disconsolate, oft refusing food and yearning only for thy presence. I beg of thee, Germanus, hurry to Ceirog and ask my father for her hand ere poor Gwladys dies of unrequited love.'

This Germanus did and with the proposed union being blessed, he arrived at Llanarmon for the nuptial ceremonies.

Following a long evening given to feasting and story-telling, many of those present, including Germanus and Winifred, became afflicted by a terrible sickness from which three of the Ceirog relatives died. And while Germanus and his sister-in-law recovered, she lost the child she was bearing.

Two years elapsed without Gwladys or her sister conceiving a child whereupon Gwladys became inconsolable believing that she was barren. Germanus, however, took a different view, there being little doubt in his own mind that their troubles were the result of Winifred and himself having been poisoned by tainted pork at the wedding, though this opinion he had long kept to himself. At last he confided his fears to Neigwl who pledged whatever assistance he could give to preserve the estate and save those who dwelled thereon from becoming bondsmen to the hated Earl of Chester.

That night, as Gwladys lay weeping in his arms, Germanus spoke with her in a fair manner confessing that while it was not impossible for her to be barren, it was more likely that his affliction had rendered him incapable of siring a sibling, adding that should he die without issue, the detested Marcher Lord may seize their lands and render her destitute. Accordingly, he bade her sleep with Neigwl in the hope that she conceived a child.

Being a dutiful wife, Gwladys slept with Neigwl, keeping their union secret from Winifred and, in time, brought forth twins who, being girls, they named Gwenabwy, after the daughter of Caw,[6] and Teleri, after the daughter of Peul.[7] When Winifred saw her sister nursing the babes, she wept continuously for seven days and seven nights, crying: 'Oh, that I could hold the child of my husband to my breast.'

Seeing her sister's misery, Gwladys spoke to Germanus saying: 'Is it not wrong for us to stand aside and see my sister die of grief when we have double that for which she yearns. Should we not, out of gratitude to Neigwl, share our happiness with them?' And to this Germanus agreed so that Winifred held her husband's child to her bosom though she did not know that Teleri was his flesh and blood.

When the christening ceremony was over and the great feast consumed, those assembled listened to Llud, the celebrated bard, as he regaled them with the glories of the past. After many such tales, which everyone had heard before, though certainly not in so splendid a manner, Germanus begged the bard to recount a new story in Gwenabwy's honour. To this, Llud responded with the Legend of the Triple Sacrifice. As the story progressed, the colour drained from Aranrhod's face, her lips began to tremble, she was seen to cross herself repeatedly until, as it reached its climax, she collapsed unconscious.

On the following morning she sent for Germanus. As he entered her room he saw that she held a crucifix in her hand which was clasped upon her heart, a phial of holy water was upon the table and a rosary lay round her neck. He waited until she had finished her prayer.

'Lo! I fear that I am upon my deathbed,' she sighed. 'Thus harken unto my words and speak nought but the truth veritable. Last night, Llud told of a woman who gave three daughters in sacrifice. Dost thou still remember her name?'

'That I do,' he replied. 'But this man speaketh in riddles for if a man cannot cast eyes upon a son, how can it be that he sired a son who could not beget a son himself?'

'Oh, Germanus! Thou art a learned man but like many others of thine ilk, thou hast not acquired the common sense to match thy scholarship. Now, in my lineage, fourteen generations have elapsed since the birth of a son. And fourteen generations have also passed since Helig, son of Llew, took unto himself a wife. And she was called Morfudd, thus named after her grandmother, wife of the great warlord, Urien Rheged, who was with King Arthur in his court at Caer Llion on Usk. And Morfudd bore seventeen sons and a daughter who was joined in the most unholy matrimony with a priest from a Druid oratory in Môn[8] by whom she bore three daughters upon the same day.' Aranrhod paused before lowering her voice: 'And the name of that woman was Cigfa!'

Germanus was taken aback. 'Art thou confessing upon thy deathbed that I am not thy husband's son?' he enquired.

'That I am not!' she returned despairingly. 'Oh, Germanus! Art thou so engrossed in thy learning that thou hast forgotten that thy father died ere thou sawest the light of day and thus could not have cast his eyes upon thee?'

'That I have not forgotten. It was that I merely placed a different interpretation upon the meaning of casting one's eyes upon a son.'

'Meanings! Interpretations! That is all one hears from philosophers!' his mother sneered. 'Tell me, my son, how dost thou interpret the conception of Gwenabwy and Teleri? As the seed of thy loins? Or didst thou give Neigwl half-a-loaf for the employment of his?'

'No less than Cigfa,' Germanus responded quietly. 'I, too, made a great sacrifice for others.'

'*Not* like Cigfa!' was his mother's angered reply. 'Thy sacrifice was in God's name! Her's was *not*! And I swear that the sacrifice thou has made for others has given me the strength to live. Go now and bring Cybi the priest to me and after I have conversed with him, beseech his assistance in overcoming thy deficiency.'

This Germanus did and later Cybi bade him and his wife make a pilgrimage to Rome that this may effect a miracle and make him fruitful again. But he was loathe to absent himself for such a long period perchance his mother died while he was away and the Earl of Chester declared the *maenolydd* to be untenanted and grant them to one of his liege men.

'Then thou must make three pilgrimages to Ynys Enlli,'[9] the priest ordained, 'this being, in God's eyes, the equal of one pilgrimage to Rome.'

'The wife of my foster-brother is likewise barren,' Germanus informed the cleric. 'If they were to make similar pilgrimages may she not also conceive?'

'With God, all things are possible,' Cybi replied. 'Go ye both alternately so that his wife may succour thy child whilst thou art away leaving thy wife to suckle her foster-child during their absence.'

And this they did, Germanus and Gwladys being the first to go. But while Neigwl and Winifred were crossing the sound from Braich y Pwll on their third journey, a great storm arose and their boat was lost, whereat Germanus and Gwladys took Teleri into their household leaving Aranrhod to acquire her eleventh *maenolydd*.

A month later, Gwladys addressed Cybi: 'Though I still weep for a child, it is for my husband's sanity that I grieve the more for he believes God hath cursed him with eternal infertility.'

'That I do understand,' the cleric replied, 'for Aranrhod advised me concerning the conception of thy children.'

'It is I who have sinned the greater,' Gwladys confessed.

'Fear not, my child,' Cybi consoled her. 'What thou didst was for love, thus thy part was not a transgression. Tell me, if he remains childless, will his grief increase?'

'Yea, father. I fear he will die of shame.'

'And would you assist him if it was within thy power?'

'There is nought I would not do to please him,' Gwladys said.

'It is perhaps God's plan that I am thy priest,' Cybi held forth. 'Long ago, I served in the Vatican as the Pontiff's train-bearer. One day, at the Seventh Station of the Cross, a great fire filled my heart on seeing which the Holy Father spake unto me: "Never have I seen the light of Heaven glow in a man's eyes as in thine today. Verily, the Holy Spirit must have entered thy Soul." Thus I knew that with God the Father, God the Son and God the Holy Ghost being as one in the Holy Trinity, I was part of God and He was part of me.'

On hearing this, Gwladys asked him if he could not then grant her a son to which he replied: 'Only God himself can ordain an Immaculate Conception yet there are other ways in which he performs His miracles. If, for thy husband's sake, thou wouldst lay with me on seven consecutive days, His Spirit will pass unto thee and thou wilt surely bear one who is a Son of God.'

This Gwladys did but, on bringing forth a child, she was smitten by puerperal fever from which she died, while Cybi's clerical garb was found floating upon the waters of Glaslyn which everyone knew was the lair of a giant Afanc.

Now with Germanus believing that the child was indeed blessed of God, he named him Cadfan in tribute to the Wisest of Kings who founded the Abbey of St Mary on Bardsey Isle. Not surprisingly, he found that the rearing of three young babes was an impossible task for a man. Unlike the custom of his day, he refused to foster his children preferring to employ a young widow named Enid, who was herself with child, as a nursemaid. When her time came she bore a girl who, being fair and beautiful was christened Olwyn. And since this woman gave all four children an equal love, Germanus decreed that Olwyn should share equally the comforts and privileges enjoyed by his own siblings.

Eventually he addressed his mother: 'Having become used to married life, I am now most lonely. Therefore I would take another wife and finding that Enid pleases me, she is the one I seek to wed.'

On hearing this, Aranrhod became doubly angered. First, because Enid was both the daughter and widow of lesser free-born

men and thus of inferior rank. And secondly because she felt that
her own son should marry a woman who could bring a twelfth
maenol as her dowry or estate.

'I understand thy concern,' Germanus protested, 'but my
children have come to love Enid as I do. Thus I fear to bring a new
woman into my household lest Enid depart and my children be
heartbroken.'

'That I do see,' his mother admitted. 'Also that a man needs the
companionship of a woman. For the sake of the children I will
strike a bargain with thee. Take this woman as a lover if thou
wilt but shouldst thou marry her I shall devise all that I
have unto thy youngest sister as an added inducement to bring
her to a prince's throne, leaving thee with nothing but thy
hendre.'

Henceforth, Germanus lived with Enid as though she was his
wife, both of them finding great happiness with their four children
who grew up as brother and sisters. Until, that is, Cadfan reached
the full bloom of manhood whereupon he said to his father: 'Lo!
As a boy I was as a brother to Olwyn. But now I am a man, I see
her as the fairest maiden in all Gwynedd and my love for her burns
through me until I can scarce eat or sleep.'

Germanus then asked Olwyn concerning her feelings to which
she replied: 'Cadfan is the most handsome and loveable man in the
realm and because of him, my eyes are blind to all things save the
sight of his countenance.'

When Aranrhod came to know of this she went into a great rage,
railing at Germanus: 'It is my will that Cadfan wed Helen, daughter
of Goronwy, for she is a comely maiden and, with her being heiress
to her father's *maenol* and he being an old man, upon my death
thou shallt at last have a commote and hold Lordship over these
territories.'

'I care little for rank or territory', Germanus declared. 'Only for
the happiness of my family and for that I will fight, to the death
if necessary.'

'Happiness! That is all the young think of these days,' his mother
snarled. 'Since thou dost not seem to possess a sense of duty, you
force me to reveal a dark secret which I prayed I may carry unto
my grave. Now, alas, I must share it with thee. Even as Gwladys
lay on her deathbed she confessed her sins to me, first because
I am more Godly than any priest and secondly, because she
had come to hate the clerics. After thou hadst returned from
thy last pilgrimage, Cybi, with double-tongued sophistry, persuaded thy wife that with the Holy Spirit having settled within

him whilst in Rome, he was now part of God and by laying
with him seven times, she would bear a Son of God.

'Thus with Cadfan being Cybi's son, thou art truly without issue
and if he be permitted to wed Olwyn, these great territories we hold
shall pass from both thy father's lineage and my own to that of
another, leaving thy sisters without the inheritance which, by right,
is now due unto them. Cadfan must be forced to wed Helen, she
being also the daughter of Indeg who is the daughter of my aunt,
Rathyen, thus ensuring that our land is retained by my family
forever.'

'Mother! There are more ways of begetting children one loves
than by lying with a woman. Gwenabwy, Teleri and Cadfan are
as much my children as any born unto man', Germanus returned
firmly.

'Then I warn thee', his mother thundered, 'if Cadfan and Olwyn
wed, I shall inform the Bishop of Llanbadarn that in order to beget
a heir, you forced Gwladys to sleep with thy foster-brother and
later with Cybi for the same purpose, afterwards drowning him in
Glaslyn. On hearing evidence of this nature, the Bishop will most
certainly up-end the candles and ex-communicate thee. So, fight to
the death, wilt thou? Whose death, Germanus? Thy own? Is it not
strange that Neigwl and Winifred also died?'

On the morrow, Germanus informed his mother that he was
making yet another pilgrimage to Bardsey Isle to expiate his sins.
This pleased the old woman greatly, she wishing him God-speed.
But instead of travelling thither, he hastened to Llyn Ogwen from
whence he ascended to Twll Du where he craved an audience with
the High Priestess, Bloddwyn.

Once ensconced within her *sanctum sanctorum*, Germanus
revealed the entire chain of events from Llud's Tale of the Triple
Sacrifice onwards, begging Bloddwyn to put a curse upon his
mother.

'If thou art to be ex-communicated for sins as trivial as thine,
does this not prove that thy god is devoid of compassion?', she
interrogated.

'I know not', Germanus replied. 'Yet I cannot believe that He
doth not possess the same love for His children that I bear unto
mine.'

'Dost thou believe that Cadfan is indeed the son of god?' she
enquired.

'Nay! That I do not believe.'

'In that thou art right', the old witch decreed. 'But not concerning
thy maker for he is a cruel god. When his son, Lucifer, displeased

him, did thy god display mercy or charity? Nay! He forsook him,
casting him into the bottomless Pit of Acheron which is known to
thee as Hell. And not only for a period of chastisement, mark thee,
but forever. Wouldst thou suffer such upon one of thy children?'

'That I would not', Germanus declared.

'Then thy god is less merciful than thou art, nor is he possessed
of half the natural love with which thou art endowed. Or any other
man! That is why we pay homage, not unto thy ruthless god, but
unto his son who, I assure thee, hath greater forbearance in his
heart than thou wilt ever find in heaven. Thus our creed is to save
humanity from the malevolence of the christian priests who do
nought but put their congregations in fear of brimstone and fire
should they fall by the wayside or display a love like thine. We,
who are despised by thy church, believe not in the agonies of ex-
communication, the brutality of the rack or other barbaric
penalties incurred by human weaknesses or love. In their place we
offer charity and absolution, asking only in return that our
followers turn from the path of idolatry as defined by thy priests.
Does that surprise thee, Germanus?'

'It is a philosophy unknown to me', he admitted.

'This being so, I will not put a curse upon thy mother', she
announced. 'Instead I will show thee a way to turn her own sanc-
timony against herself. When Llud recounted his tale, this was
incomplete for the most important aspect was unknown to him.
The remainder I know well for one of my forebears was present
that day upon Moel Siabod.'

At this, she acquainted Germanus with the final chapter of the
saga and, after instructing him to pass this on to Llud, she opened
a large, wooden chest from which she took three identical sets of
bracelets and ropes of pearls.

'These, I assure thee, are not the ones plundered from the
tumulus, though they are similar. Take them and follow my
ordinances faithfully whereupon thy happiness and that of thy
children shall be assured.'

After receiving these instructions, Germanus returned to his
home.

In celebration of his mother's seventieth birthday, Germanus
held a great feast and, when this had been consumed, Llud enter-
tained everyone with many new stories. At last he addressed
Aranrhod.

'My lady! Over twenty years have passed since I regaled thee
with the Tale of the Triple Sacrifice. Alas, in my youth, the full
report was not known to me but I have now remedied that defect.'

And with that he launched into the tale as told before but, on concluding that episode, continued thus:

'One Easter Monday, some years later, the tumulus was plundered, the skeletons and jewellery being carried off, a deed which many attributed to church priests. This, however, was not so. Almost immediately, the sun ceased to shine and, once more, bad weather prevailed.

'The Druids again assembled on Moel Siabod, remaining there for forty days and forty nights when great thunderings and lightning rent the skies, following which they descended to the vale, saying that a voice had spoken unto them. And this is what they heard: that if ever the three sets of adornments were reunited with the reincarnated souls of the three sacrificial virgins, the first person to see all three maidens wearing them would be the reincarnated desecrator of the tumulus. Then, with the guilty one revealed, the Gods would exact retribution in full, consigning the culprit to the bottomless Pit of Acheron for ever.

'Only when this punishment had been enacted would the Gods relent.'

A week later, Gwenabwy took her place at the breakfast table. 'Look what Enid has given me as a birthday present,' she enthused pointing to the gold clasp set with flashing garnets upon her wrist and the rope of pearls around her neck.

As Aranrhod recognized the design her lips began to tremble, the colour drained from her cheeks and rigors shook her entire frame.

'Take them off!' she commanded. 'Give them back at once! Those who wear adornments which have been placed on pagan bodies given in sacrifice will have the mark of the cloven foot upon them till they die!'

'No!' Gwenabwy answered. 'I'm going to keep them . . . and wear them every day . . . forever! And so is Teleri. Enid gave her a set as well. And she's got another set, she says, locked away in a box, though she's never looked at them in her life.'

Aranrhod rose unsteadily and, after crossing herself thrice, she held her crucifix before her as she left the room, making her way hurriedly along the track towards Beddkelert. As she came to the bridge spanning the outflow of Llyn Mymbyr, she saw a maiden resembling Teleri some distance ahead. Instantly, she crossed the bridge and entered the forest on the western slopes of Moel Siabod. No sooner had she done so than she espied the same girl behind her. She darted from the pathway but, as she hid behind a huge oak tree, another maiden called to her within the depths of the forest. 'Why hidest thou from us, grandmother?'

'Kelert preserve me,'[10] Aranrhod prayed out loud.

Trembling with fear, the old woman returned to the path and made her way upwards towards the Rowan copse where another voice greeted her. 'Greetings, grandmother!'

Raising her eyes, she saw Teleri standing before her with a bracelet of gold and flashing garnets upon her outstretched wrist and a rope of pearls about her neck.

'Take off those baubles!' she screamed. 'They were fashioned by the Devil himself.'

'That I shall not,' Teleri replied. 'Enid gave them to me as a birthday present and I'm going to keep them . . . and wear them every day . . . forever!'

Teleri advanced upon her grandmother. 'Why dost thou flinch from these, oh woman of God?' she taunted.

'Stand aside!' Aranrhod screeched breathlessly. 'Before the Furies consume the pair of us!' And with that she held her crucifix aloft but as she raced past her grand-daughter, the thin, gold chain caught upon a Buckthorne tearing the cross from her hand and catapulting it high into a Hawthorne tree. Undeterred, she raced up the mountainside, her heart pounding with every step until she reached the summit where she lay exhausted.

At length she heard a maiden's voice and, opening her eyes, saw Olwyn kneeling beside her, swathed from head to foot in a woollen shawl. 'What afflicts thee, grandmother?' Olwyn asked gently.

'Gwenabwy and Teleri have artefacts of the Devil upon their wrists and Haloes of Hell about their necks,' she wept. 'The same as were plundered from the grave of the Three Sacrificial Virgins. Woe is me that my grandchildren are in the clutches of Lucifer.'

'Come, grandmother, raise thyself and I will accompany thee to thy home', Olwyn proffered.

But as Aranrhod rose, the shawl slipped from Olwyn's shoulders revealing a gold clasp with flashing garnets upon her wrist and a rope of pearls about her neck.

'Get thee hence from me!' Aranrhod screamed. 'Thou, Teleri and Gwenabwy are the Triumvirate of the Devil Incarnate!'

'Hold thy tongue, old woman,' Olwyn retaliated. 'Thou art nothing but the reincarnation of the one who desecrated the tumulus wherein the bodies of Cigfa's daughters once lay!'

On hearing these dread words, Aranrhod's eyes glazed, she flung her arms wide as in a cross, moaning fearfully, and then fell to the ground.

When Olwyn reached Llyn Mymbyr, Germanus, Enid, Cadfan and his two sisters were waiting at the bridge.

'It has come to pass,' she declared. 'Aranrhod is dead.'

'Nay,' Cadfan replied. 'Look yonder at the crest.'

As they turned, they saw Aranrhod stand erect and raise her arms to Heaven as though in supplication. Even as she did so a loud rumbling echoed in the bowels of the mountains, increasing in intensity until the very summit of Moel Siabod exploded and the once smooth surface became a tumbling mass of shattered rocks. And from the very highest point a pillar of purple smoke rose forth as in a plume, its very colour proclaiming that it could only have risen from the bottomless Pit of Acheron in the manner which Bloddwyn foretold.

Following this intercession, Aranrhod was never seen again, Germanus inheriting the eleven *maenolydd*, of which he gave one each to Gwenabwy and Teleri, three to Cadfan and retained six for himself. Thus the family holding never became a *commote* and neither did any of the girls wed princes.

And this is the end of Mhaira's First Wondertale.

True or false? Who can tell but it should be borne in mind that in the 6th century it was possible to walk from North Wales to Cumbria across what is now part of the Irish sea. Subsequently, major geographical subsidences in the sea-bed occurred coupled with corresponding upheavals of the land mass. It was probably one of the latter which resulted in Moel Siabod's shining dome disintegrating into a tumultuous mass of boulders with a consequential cloud of dust (rather than a plume of purple smoke) rising into the sky.

Such a phenomenon would be quickly seized upon by the bards to embellish more mundane tales with a supernatural aura. Even in the 19th century a mining geologist wrote (of Siabod): 'The terrible peak of this lonesome outpost of Nature is the Epitomy of Confusion. While there is no evidence of volcanic activity, the rocks are in such a state of Turmoil that this can hardly be the result of normal Erosion. Thus I am forced to believe that an upheaval of Gargantuan proportions burst the Superstratum, hurling it high into the Heavens from whence it descended in a Develish disorder.'

It is also historically correct that during the 8th century England and Wales suffered from seven years of almost interminable rain, this being followed by 14 years which were the best 'memory could recall'.

Thus it is likely that Mhaira's Wondertale was based upon a true family incident which led to a most happy ending with love being triumphant over greed. At the same time, she undoubtedly used this as a vehicle to project witches in a far better light than that in which they were usually regarded.

The Legend of the Triple Sacrifice also crops up in the West Riding of Yorkshire, the sacrifice supposedly taking place within the ancient Druids Circle of Rombald's Moor, and with the self-same supernatural element being exploited to resolve a similar family feud centered on Soyland Moor in the late 1700's.

Since the Mhaira of Devil's Elbow would never have ventured near Soyland Moor (where neither Saint nor Satan dared to tread), the inference is that the 'legend' was introduced to Yorkshire by Cistercian monks who had fled from Gwynedd and subsequently founded both Fountains and Rievaulx Abbeys in that county. (See the warning received by the original Mhaira in 'Owain Gwynedd's Silver Dagger'.) Since the monks were noted for having committed Gwyneddan legends to the written word, this would explain why the two versions of the legend were preserved with such unique accuracy.

Thus the likelihood is that this is a true Wondertale, *viz*: a mixture of truth and unexplained supernatural, together with a final embellishment given to it by Mhaira in a most bard-like manner.

THE THREE SISTERS OF ARDUDWY

(A.D. 1062)

A medieval romance which those who dwelled in Cwm Artro and the village of Llandbedr conveniently 'forgot', perchance any subsequent investigation by the authorities into what, at first sight, appeared to be a tragic accident, revealed that it was a most gruesome murder.

In the 11th century, Gwynedd was ruled by the bastard Gruffydd ap Llewelyn. Although he was strong and vigorously opposed the Saxon hordes, his reign was the most ruthless the Principality had experienced since the dark days of Maelgwn. Thus sorrow was mixed with relief when he was slain by Harold's army in 1063.

He was succeeded by the rightful ruler, Gruffydd ap Cynan, whose mother was the daughter of a Viking king. Three years later the Normans swept through England before turning upon Wales in a three-pronged campaign. Their northern army was commanded by the redoubtable Hugh of Avranches against whose armoured troops the Welsh stood little chance, being forced back until Gruffydd was compelled to seek exile in Ireland where he remained until 1135.

Two years later he was succeeded by his son, Owain Gwynedd, who kept a low profile until the death of King Henry I in 1142. Succession to the English throne was then hotly disputed by Stephen and the Empress Matilda, the resultant internal power struggle giving Owain the opportunity to reconquer Gwynedd.

Over the years he effected a series of clever marriages, not only for himself but also in respect of his children, and by this means held the Welsh together in such unaccustomed unity and strength that he was able to preserve peace between Gwynedd and England for 25 years.

Now Owain was credited with having sired no less than 19 princes and this story concerns two of them. Unfortunately, in the various reports concerning the Battle of Corwen and its aftermath, there is some confusion as to their identities. After careful research, the names attributed to them by Mhaira appear to be the correct ones and the University College of Wales does not dispute her facts.

Hywel ap Enion was a devout and kindly man. Since he was both handsome and the most important wool merchant in Llanbedr, the maidens of Ardudwy were forever casting their eyes in his direction but none possessed the qualities he considered essential in a wife.

Shortly before reaching his fortieth year he met a childless widow named Ruth whose life had hitherto been one of unhappiness. As the daughter of a Jewish banker from Shrewsbury, she was raised in comfort but on being orphaned at eighteen, found that her father's debts reduced her to penury.

She at once realized that in order to avoid privation she must marry but not being the comeliest of maidens and having no dowry, the young men of substance avoided her, only a handful of impoverished Gentile fishermen showing any inclination to take her as a bride. It was not long, however, before a rich and ardent suitor appeared albeit that he was a widower of forty winters whose wife had borne him three daughters but no sons. And while he was hardly the acme of Ruth's matrimonial aspirations, she was determined to regain the opulent life to which she was accustomed.

Before a year was up she discovered that the honeyed words with which he had wooed her were merely a trap to acquire the means of producing an heir. Thus when the marriage did not prove fruitful, he treated his young wife as little better than a servant, and upon his death left the bulk of his fortune to his daughters.

In Ruth, Hywell found all the attributes dearest to him and with his love for her being requited, they married and found great happiness together in their *hafod* at Pen-y-bont in Cwm Artro. Over the years, Ruth bore three children whom they named Sophia, meaning wisdom; Rebecca, that is, of enchanting beauty; and Gwen, white and fair. When Sophia was fourteen her mother contracted a dread disease. Upon her deathbed she implored Hywel to honour the tradition of her faith that the eldest daughter be married before the second, who should likewise wed before the third, whereat he swore on the memories of St Patrick and Moses that he would respect her wishes.

The sisters grew up as unlike each other as could be imagined. While Rebecca was comely and dark-eyed, Gwen, with her fair complexion, blue eyes and hair as yellow as broom, was famed as the most beauteous and best endowed maiden in Ardudwy. But whereas Rebecca was of a pleasant disposition, her younger sister displayed an increasing vanity and an utter abhorrence of everything which was imperfect.

It was Sophia, however, who having inherited her mother's traits, was Hywel's favourite. Not only was she well-versed in philosophy, poetry and history but was gifted musically, being proficient upon the harp and having the ability to compose ballads of rare quality which she sang in the sweetest of voices. Added to which she had a sympathetic nature and was learned in the arts of preparing herbal medications to heal the sick. Yet Sophia was the heaviest cross Hywel had to bear for she was as ugly as Gwen was beautiful to the extent that everyone who saw her face recoiled in horror.

One day, as Prince Rhydderch and Prince Dylan were returning from a deer-hunt on the sharp crest of Craig y Saeth,[1] they came upon Rebecca and Gwen who were seated by the Afon Artro. Rhydderch ventured a greeting.

'And God prosper thee as well,' Rebecca answered as she turned towards him.

When Rhydderch saw her countenance he reigned abruptly, for of all the maidens he had ever seen, she was the most beautiful.

'Fair lady,' he addressed her. 'Pray acquaint me with thy name for until I know it, I swear that I shall never again sleep in peace.'

'I am Rebecca, daughter of Hywel ap Enion, and this is my sister, Gwen. And a plague upon thee, sire, if thou dost think we are wanton wenches disporting ourselves in an unseemly manner,' she returned somewhat tartly.

'My lady! I am Rhydderch and this, my brother, is named Dylan, and I assure you that, being sons of Owain Gwynedd, we are the most valorous of men and not, as you seem to fear, the despoilers of virtue.'

At this introduction they both turned towards the others who were as statues, seeing only each other, their eyes entranced by the wonderment of love. At last Dylan spoke: 'By my faith, I now recall how Olwyn of Dolwyddelan foretold that should a Prince of the Realm hunt for three days upon Craig y Saeth without a hart succumbing to his arrows, unless he bathed forthwith in the waters of Llyn Morwynion he would himself succumb to the next hart he met.

'Fairest maiden, that prophecy has come to pass. For three days I have led the chase on yonder crag and ne'er a hart did I see. But now, having failed to bath in the Lake of the Maidens, I have indeed succumbed to the next one I have met. And that is thy heart, dear lady.'

Without deflecting her eyes Gwen answered him: 'Fair prince, I am a chaste maiden and beg thee not to tarnish thy shining image by wooing me discourteously with false words.'

'That I do not,' Dylan replied. 'Rather, if thou dost requite my love, pray take me unto thy father that I may ask for thee.'

'That I will do most willingly', she returned softly, whereupon Rhydderch began to hold forth:

'Fairest Rebecca! I, too, confess that this day I have been smitten by a love which burns within me like unto a fire and, shouldst thou find me as pleasant to thine eye as thou art to mine, take me also thither that I may likewise ask for thy hand.'

Gwen turned as though to lead them to the *hafod* but Rebecca restrained her. 'Be not consumed by the passion of the moment,' she cautioned. 'My princes, I bid thee depart and leave us to take counsel with our father. Then, in seven days, if thou art of the same minds, return and ask for us.'

When the princes had departed, Gwen chided her sister for sending them away.

'Fear not,' Rebecca assured her. 'There is good reason why I despatched them. Had they returned with us they would have come upon Sophia and perchance considered that with the traits of the forefathers passing even unto the third generation, the children we bear may be afflicted with countenances as ill-contrived as that of our poor sister. Then we would have lost them forever.'

When they arrived home Gwen could not suppress her excitement. 'I am to marry a prince!' she burst forth. 'And so is Rebecca! Seven days hence, Dylan and Rhydderch, sons of the illustrious Owain Gwynedd, are to come hither and ask for us.'

'Count not thy blessings before the ewe has been well served,' Sophia warned.

'Thy words are nought but jealousy,' Gwen reprimanded haughtily. 'Thou wilt never be a princess with thy face! Nor, indeed, become any man's wife!'

'Neither will thee nor Rebecca until Sophia weds,' her father retorted, whereupon he informed them of the pledge he had given to their mother concerning the order in which they may be married.

'Then a husband must be found for her,' Gwen insisted, 'for I swear that our mother never intended us to remain maidens all our lives!'

'Have patience,' Hywel declared. 'Sophia will marry. Yet I shall not give her to any man save he whom she chooses of her own free will.'

'Then, dear father,' Gwen pleaded, 'pray do not thwart our chances but, instead, hide Sophia when they come to pay us court lest they fear that our children will be likewise afflicted and thus spurn us.'

'That I will do,' he answered. 'But mark my words, one day Sophia will meet a man who, seeing the beauty of her soul, shall be blind to the imperfections of her countenance and, with his love being greater than riches or rank, shall win her hand in matrimony.'

At this, Gwen swept out of the room but Rebecca remained and said to her father: 'I care not that Rhydderch is a prince. I would gladly wed him if he was but a poor fisherman such is the love I bear him. Help me in my travail, I beg of you.'

On the seventh day the two princes returned to ask for the maidens' hands to which Hywel agreed subject to Sophia being married the first. And this the princes accepted as being the redemption of a holy pledge.

Rebecca's love for Rhydderch grew until she could wait no longer and, at the end of the third month, she slept with him. And because she had not known a man before, on the following morning he enquired of her what she would have as her maiden-fee. Thus she bade him commission Sophia to compose a great ballad commemorating his father's epic deeds during the first twenty-five years of his reign, following which he should let it be known that any man who could win Sophia's hand and bring her to his father's *caer* as court harpist would be rewarded beyond his wildest dreams.

And this Rhydderch did, so that a multitude of young men flocked to Pen-y-bont intent upon marrying Sophia but such was their distress upon seeing her countenance that they all departed instantly. At length, a blind man arrived at the *hafod* and asked to hear Sophia's great ballad. As her fingers plucked at the strings of her harp, a powerful air, descriptive of Owain's enthronement resounded through the entire room. Then the tempo changed and Sophia's melodious voice launched into a pastoral giving thanks for the 25 years of peace which their prince had brought them. Finally the music throbbed in a grand bravura until it streamed from the open window and soared to the mountains above. As the ballad ended, tears ran from the man's sightless eyes whereat he asked for her hand.

'How canst thou, a blind man, support a wife?' Hywel asked.

'Fair sire! Prince Rhydderch has offered a fortune to anyone who will bring thy daughter to his father's *caer* as court harpist and as a wife.'

'How can I be certain that it is not the reward thou seekest rather than my daughter's heart?' Hywel probed.

'Did I not weep when I heard her sing with the sweetest voice in all the world?'

'Then accompany me to Llandanwy Church and there, before the priest, kneel at the stone of St Patrick, swearing that it is truly my daughter's heart you seek rather than the reward, likeway praying that if you have borne false witness in your declaration, may both your legs break when you rise from your knees.'

But the man refused and departed, following which no other suitors came to Pen-y-bont.

Seeing that her sister's plan had failed, Gwen decided that the situation demanded action of the greatest import. Thus she slept with Dylan who, finding that she was a maiden, asked her what she would have as her maiden fee. And the fee she named was as follows: 'That upon the next full moon he should arrange for Sophia to be abducted and carried off to the summit of Mynydd Llanbedr where her captors should bind her to a stake and then set three ravenous wolves upon her. When all trace of her was gone, save for her apparel, the ropes and stakes should be removed leaving no trace of human involvement.'

At this Dylan was sorely troubled. Failure to discharge the obligation of a maiden-fee was considered a great dishonour, yet he could not bring himself to perform this wicked deed. But after pondering awhile, his dilemma was resolved by no less a personage than the King of England.

King Henry II was a brash young man of thirty years and the most odious of the Angevins. As the ruler of all the lands from the Scottish border to the Pyrenees with the exception of Wales, he was greatly angered that the Welsh Princes refused to pay homage to him. Accordingly, in 1164, he mustered a large army at Oswestry made up of the finest English troops with others from Flanders, Gascony, Anjou and Normandy.

Fortunately for the Welsh, a great oak forest stood between the invading army and the Ceirog river forcing Henry to employ woodcutters to clear a passage. This gave the Welsh princes time to assemble their warriors and, for the first time in history, the entire nation stood together. Owain Gwynedd's men kept watch, drawing the enemy towards Corwen and, during their march, Rhydderch and Dylan led raiding parties against them in such a series of murderous ambushes that, in order to prevent any repetition, the King pitched his camp on the notorious Moel-y-Gwynt (The Windy Hill). Owain, with his knowledge of the terrain, bivouacked his host in the sheltered Dee valley, despatching the men of Ceirog to prevent any supplies reaching his adversaries.

For days on end, violent storms raged over the mountains and prevented Henry from mounting an attack. At length, with his supplies running low, he was forced to lead his bedraggled men in a retreat to England, suffering greatly as Dylan played havoc with his baggage train.

On his return to London, Henry vowed to avenge what was seen as a notable defeat and planned reprisals against his foes. Armed bands of agents were despatched to infiltrate the Welsh countryside where they succeeded in taking Rhydderch and Dylan, together with two of their sisters, as hostages. To the south, other bands carried off two of Rhys ap Gruffydd's sons and having ensconced their captives in an English castle, tormented the males in a most gruesome fashion, inflicting the worst of their hideous brutalities upon Dylan as retribution for the grievous losses which his men had inflicted upon Henry's army. Eventually, when they tired of their amusement, the captors bound the maidens to heavy chairs and, after stuffing their ears, forcing them to watch as they slowly and agonizingly blinded the two princes before leaving them unconscious and roped together on Offa's Dyke.

Rhydderch and his brother sought sanctuary at Hywel's home, Dylan being borne there on a litter of wattle. When Gwen saw her lover's shattered body and bloodied sockets from which eyes of blue had once entranced her, she recoiled from his presence and departed to her aunt's home at Caergynog in Cwm Nantcol. Thus Sophia was left to minister unto Dylan's needs while Rebecca nursed Rhydderch.

The winter passed and had it not been for Sophia's medicinal knowledge and constant attention, Dylan would surely have died. But as the glades turned green and the drifts of spring flowers scented the warm air, he took his first faltering steps guided by Sophia's and her father's unerring hands. Little by little she encouraged him to venture further until, on Summer's Day, he mounted his horse which Sophia led to Llyn Cwm Bychan.

There they dismounted, leaving their horses at the ancestral home of the Llywyds. Then she took his arm, guiding him slowly up the pack-horse track rising through Bwlch Tyddiadd, pausing constantly to savour the sweet smell of wild thyme, harebells and tormentil. When they reached the summit of the pass, they turned eastwards until they sat together on the bank of Llyn Morwynion.

After they had taken of their repast, Dylan broke the silence: 'Many have been the nights when I have thanked God for sending thee unto me and preserving me from the hand of Death. Now, as I sit here, I can understand why the maidens of Clwyd, after being abducted by the men of Ardudwy, flung themselves into these dark waters, preferring to drown rather than be torn from those they had come to love. That is how I now feel.'

'Oh, Dylan, 'tis a grievous hurt which Gwen hath done unto thee. Cast her from thy mind, I prithee, for until you do, you shall never sleep in peace again.'

'Ah, sweetest Sophia,' he replied, 'it is not for Gwen that I yearn: it is for mine eyes. If thou couldst have given me back my sight as thou hast resurrected my body, then I would kneel before thee, declaring my love, and ask thy father for thy hand in marriage.'

'If eyes thou hadst, then thou would likewise have fled from my company as others have before thee.'

'Nay, my dearest,' Dylan proclaimed, 'eyes see but the attraction of the flesh: without them I have not been blinded to the beauty of thy soul.'

'That my father has often said I possess,' Sophia admitted, 'but I know that I am the ugliest of all women, *sans* beauty of countenance, *sans* love, *sans* dowry.'

'My love,' Dylan answered softly. 'Thou hast a dowry beyond rubies or gold. Thy dowry is a heart as pure and good as ever beat. Oh, that I possessed my eyes and could lead thee through life.'

And from what Dylan had said, Sophia knew that he truly loved her and that her father's prophecy had come to pass for, at last, she had found a man who cared not for riches or rank but beheld only the beauty of her soul.

'Were that I was comely so that men did not avert their eyes from my countenance,' she said sadly. 'Then, willingly, would I become thine eyes and lead thee through life.'

Dylan took her hand and pressed it to his lips. 'I care not what others see or think', he told her. 'I want thee for thyself for my love is greater than all other things. I prithee, Sophia, marry me and bear my children, bringing happiness not only to both of us but to Rhydderch and Rebecca as well, for so great is her love for him that she has already consented to be his bride if thou wilt first be mine.'

And as Cwm Artro shone resplendently in the golden glow of September, Sophia married Dylan and Rhydderch wed Rebecca, all four living happily ever after.

As for Gwen, she never did become a Princess, nor for that matter did any man ever pay court to her again. But one day, some years later, her torn and bloodstained clothing was found on Mynydd Llanbedr. And it was whispered that on the previous night, three spectral wolves were seen upon the summit, howling a fearful lament in the yellow light of an August moon.

And that is the end of Mhaira's Second Wondertale.

Fact or fiction? The historical aspect of the story is undeniably correct, including Henry's dastardly deed. So why should the romantic element — an oasis of love and humanity set amid one of the cruellest period known to mankind — not also be true? At least, I think it is!

THE MAIDENS OF THE SEA MARSH

incorporating
'Maelgwn & the Yellow Beast' and 'The Afanc'
(A.D. 1062)

During the early part of the 6th century, Wales consisted of four
small and sparsely populated 'kingdoms'. Their rulers, who in reality were little more than tribal leaders, bore the exalted title of
Prince. North Wales, which was variously known as Arfon or
Gwynedd, was ruled by Maelgwn Gwynedd, the 'Island Dragon',
a mighty warrior who, it was said 'closed his ears to the music of
Heaven and listened only to the flattery of the bards'. As time went
by, he became a self-centred and power-crazed tyrant whose burning ambition was to become Brenhin Pennaf, that is, the Chief King
of all Wales.

In an attempt to realize his ambition he challenged the other
princes to a contest designed to prove which of them was the most
courageous and, at the same time, show who possessed the greatest
power over the elements, cleverly adding that if his invitation was
rejected, this would be regarded as a display of cowardice.

Being unable to ignore such a taunt, they all agreed to sit upon their
thrones in the Dovey estuary when the Spring tide ran highest, and
whoever was able to withstand the awesome power of the sea would
become Brenhin Pennaf. Unbeknown to the others, Maelgwn equip-
ped his throne with inflated pigskins concealed beneath a coverlet of
figured cordwain so that when the swirling tide began to engulf the
three other princes, he floated easily upon the waves while they fled
towards the river-bank in fear of their lives.

'Lo!' Maelgwn mocked them. 'Dost thou not see how I ride upon
the ocean and have dominion over it? Thus am I not the noblest
among us?'

And all who were present marvelled at Maelgwn, making
obeisance before him and declaring that he was surely Brenhin
Pennaf.

In those far off days, life in Gwynedd was a rigorous one and the
people were used to having oppressive rulers but, with supreme
power having gone to Maelgwn's head, he soon exceeded the worst

25

depredatiions they had ever experienced. At Deganwy, he built a great *caer*[1] wherein he surrounded himself with a band of fawning lackeys who were more than willing to share his life of drunkenness and debauchery and participate in orgies too terrible to relate.

His subjects lived in constant fear of their lives, forever praying for deliverance but they were powerless to overthrow him or even speak ill of their prince, such was the number of informers he sent amongst them. His lust knew no bounds and to satiate this he assumed *droit de seigneur* thus giving himself the right to sleep with any maiden on the night prior to her wedding day. Later, he extended this authority to widows, and it was reported that if he saw a beautiful, young wife who had previously escaped his attention, her unfortunate husband was arrested, charged with treason and hung, whereupon Maelgwn would announce to the widow that she was greatly honoured by being allowed to share his bedchamber.

Eventually a man named Taliesin arose. Legend had it that he was the son of Prince Tegid, born of many fruits, flowers, earth, and water from the 9th wave and who, as a babe, had been cast in a coracle upon the Dyfi tide and washed ashore at Conwy where he was fostered by a king. Even as a stripling he astonished everyone by his wisdom, becoming a poet and the greatest bard of all. In time, he began to prophesy and his foretellings invariably came to fruition.

In the year A.D. 547, Taliesin journeyed to the summit of the Llanberis Pass from whence he climbed into the mountain fastness of Snowdon, closeting himself in a cave set in the sheer face of Lliwedd. There he contemplated for seven days and seven nights before descending to Arfon where he prophesied that 'ere the oxen had trodden the grain from the ears of corn, a great beast would arise from the depths of the Sea Marsh of The Maidens, its hair, teeth and glaring eyes all as yellow as the gorse which flowered by Llyn Llydaw. And before the women completed the winnowing of the grain and chaff, this monster would avenge the dishonour which Maelgwn had inflicted upon the Maidens of The Land, thus freeing Gwynedd from the yoke of its oppressor.

About this time, the Yellow Plague was ravaging the whole of Europe and it was not long before it crossed the channel and spread northwards with great rapidity, reaching Gwynedd by late summer.

Fearful for his life, Maelgwn and a few of his liege men isolated themselves in his *caer*, sealing the doors and gateways against all others. For a time it appeared that they had escaped the dreaded pestilence. Then, one day, a maiden's voice — sweeter by far than any Maelgwn had ever heard before — called his name from outside the walls of his palace. Being in his cups and having been denied a woman's company for many weeks, he lurched to the gate and peered through the keyhole. Almost immediately, he clutched at his vitals and fell, convulsed with pain, his last words being: 'The Yellow Beast!'

Two of Maelgwn's lackeys rushed to his assistance while the remainder clambered upon the ramparts but all they saw was a trail of huge three-clawed footprints leading down to the sea. On descending to the courtyard they found that both their companions were dead. Knowing that if they touched the bodies they would likewise become victims, they deliberated concerning the disposal of the corpses. At length, they piled brushwood over the bodies creating a funeral pyre, so all that remained of Maelgwn was his ashes. And it was said that following the triple death, not a single other person was afflicted by the plague.

Thereafter, Maelgwn's successor, perhaps remembering the supernatural power of the Sea Maidens, ruled in a fair manner, with his subjects rejoicing in their newly found freedom.

In A.D. 554, a new terror struck the good people who dwelled in the Vale of Conwy between Bettws-y-Coed and the Afon Lledr. One day, a young maiden vanished unaccountably, and by the time the next moon had waxed and waned, another disappeared without trace. A month later while Owein Barfog[2], the riverkeeper, was working on his nets near Clogwyn Brith, he espied a maiden approach the river whereupon she removed her buskins in order to bathe her feet. As she did so, a huge beast emerged from the Great Pool and confronted her.

The appearance of the creature was so grotesque that it rendered the river-keeper incapable of movement or speech, for while it had three eyes set within a head no larger than a man's, its yellowish-green body was the size of seven oxen, with three powerful hindlegs and three arms, all terminating in three-clawed fingers. As he watched, transfixed, the creature began to sing in the sweetest voice he had ever heard. The girl made no move to escape and as the beast pressed its head against her breast and caressed her body with the tenderness of a lover, she responded willingly to its touch.

Eventually, when the creature took hold of her hand and slid back into the pool, the maiden followed without demur until they both disappeared from sight, the only evidence remaining being her buskins which Owein gathered up before hastening to Bettws-y-Coed where he related the incident to The Elders.

Since Owein was a bard and harpist of the highest repute who not only held a most coveted position of trust as the river-keeper but was also known to be intolerant of false witness, The Elders accepted his story without reservation. As they considered his report, one old sage recalled that in days of yore a similar monster once inhabited Cadair yr Aur Frychin[3] from where it continuously ensnared young men into a hollow beneath the banks of the lake. One day, having been lured from its watery lair, it was seen to be an *Afanc*[4] from the Other World, whereupon it was hunted up the Bwlch Drws-y-Coed and killed.

Another white-beard dug more deeply into the past. He recollected that after an enormous beast took up its abode in Llyn Ffynnon Las,[5] sheep and goats had vanished mysteriously each night until Hu the Mighty hauled it from the lake and slew it. That, too, proved to be an *Afanc* from the Other World.

In view of this evidence, The Elders considered that what Owein had seen was also an *Afanc* whose advent may well have a bearing upon a rumour which had been circulating for some time. This hinted that several of the Sea Maidens were now too old to fulfil their duties and, as *Morynion* (Maidens), being sworn to celibacy and thus unable to multiply, their matriarch was anxious to increase their numbers.

With this in mind, The Elders came to the conclusion that this Afanc was almost certainly the same one which the Sea Maidens despatched to end Maelgwn's notorious reign and, in so doing, freed their Sisters of the Land from the fearful defilements to which the tyrant subjected them. Now, it was argued, they were demanding tribute for their intercession.

There were those who argued that the beast should be slain but the majority felt that this would anger the Sea Maidens so greatly that they might inflict a chastisement upon the Principality even worse than the Yellow Plague itself. Furthermore, since the indemnity was being limited to only one maiden per moon, and which would probably not last overlong, it was considered that this was a far less burden for the womenfolk to bear than had been their lot under Maelgwn. Accordingly, The Elders decided to let matters take their own course, Owein being sworn to silence on pain of being struck dumb.

The Elders optimism was short lived. Thereafter, each Sabbath, another maiden vanished, so that by the third full moon, no less than seven were missing from their homes, including Owein's favourite niece. The Elders then consulted the priest who, in order to avoid outraging the Maidens, advocated a compromise solution, that is, to inform everyone that a Devil's Disciple was abroad, on account of which, the womenfolk were forbidden to venture near the Great Pool.

This blatant distortion of the truth angered Owein beyond all measure, instantly destroying his erstwhile faith in the priesthood. Next day he set forth to visit the Witches' Coven of Twll Du where he knew that the High Priestess possessed powers beyond the ken of mere mortals. On his arrival there he recounted the entire story from Maelgwn's death onwards.

'I prithee, High Priestess,' he concluded, 'cast a spell upon the *Afanc* and in return for this boon I shall sing thy praises from Caer Fyrddin[6] unto Afon Dyfrdwy.'[7]

The witch regarded Owein acutely before replying. 'What thou hast seen,' she said, 'was not a mythical *Afanc* but a *Tridactyl*, thus named because it possesses three arms, legs, fingers and eyes. A millenium ago, long before Bran waded from Wales to Ireland, these creatures were commonplace, and there were many reports that they lived on human flesh, preferring that of young maidens whom they seduced before feasting upon their bodies. Some still exist, one often being sighted under the lee of Mynydd Bannawg.[8]

'As for the Sea Maidens and *Afancs*, they are nothing but *mithos*[9] perpetuated by Christian priests to put the adherents of thy faith in perpetual fear of *Annwyn*.[10]. If thy god was as omnipotent as thy priests declare, there could be no place for others whom they fear to be more powerful than their own.

'Return ye unto thy *dinas* and seek out the two most valiant young men, and after dipping the tips of their spears and flights of arrows in poison, slay the beast.

'Then when thou hast delivered Arfon of this scourge, it will be thy praises they shall sing, not only in the two vales but from Môn[11] to Pengwern.[12] Following this, return here and be bathed in the Lake of Absolution below whereupon we shall instruct thee well concerning our Master and The Truth.'

Owein immediately returned to Betws-y-Coed but neither spears nor arrows could pierce the *Afanc's* scales, nor could they reach his eyes which it covered with its horny hands.

When the *Afanc* found that he was being denied the female companionship for which he increasingly craved, he waxed angry and created a terrible tempest at the mouth of the Conwy estuary. This caused tidal wave after tidal wave to sweep up the Afon Conwy until the 9th wave, greater in height than seven men, inundated the entire vale, ruining the crops, flooding the homes and destroying half the cattle and sheep.

Not realizing the true reason for the *Afanc's* wrath, The Elders revealed the beast's existence to everyone, appealing for information concerning any untoward deed which may have angered it. That same evening, an old woman approached them saying that she had seen three men by the Great Pool, one firing arrows, another hurling spears and a third directing them. The latter, she stated, was the bearded river-keeper whom she had also seen recently leaving the Devil's Coven at Twll Du.

Owein was brought before The Elders' Court where he was charged with consorting with *wrâchs*[13] and also breaking his solemn vow of silence. At first he denied everything but under the threat of having boiling lead poured in his ears, he admitted revealing the existence of the beast to the High Priestess and leading the attempt upon its life.

In his defence Owein pleaded that the beast was not an *Afanc* at all but a *Tridactyl* which first seduced young maidens and then feasted upon them but The Elders scorned this, holding that only an *Afanc* would have the power to control the elements and create a tempest of hitherto unknown proportions.

'Didst thou not swear upon the threat of being struck dumb that thou wouldst hold thy tongue concerning the *Afanc*?' the Chief Elder interrogated.

Owein remained silent. Then the Elder spoke again: 'Thou hast broken thy bond of silence and by so doing brought the wrath of the Sea Maidens upon our land. Henceforth thou shalt never need to hold thy tongue again for dumb thou shalt be forever.'

And with that, they cut out Owein's tongue and threw him into a deep dungeon.

Now that the danger had become public knowledge, a general outcry rose up for The Elders to take whatever action was necessary to ensure the womenfolks' safety. The young men were particularly vehement, openly stating that if the white-beards could not deal with the problem, it was time they were replaced by others who were not in their dotage.

As it had already been demonstrated that they were incapable of slaying the *Afanc*, The Elders decided that it must be moved to a lake where it would be unable to wreak its spite upon anyone and since the loss of a few goats and sheep was infinitely preferable to the loss of any more maidens, they chose Glaslyn — leagues distant and high in the mountain amphitheatre beneath Lliwedd, Yr Wydffa and Crib Goch.

Carpenters were instructed to make a huge sledge with great hoops of iron on all four sides, and while they laboured, a smith prepared strong chains, with every link forged. When all was ready, the sledge was placed in a shallow trench near the edge of the Great Pool and covered by a thin layer of sand. Next, the chains were secured to one side of the sledge and then held aloft in the form of an archway by thin ropes, the free ends being run through the hoops on the opposite side where they were fastened to ropes which terminated in the trees where men waited. Finally, the arch was camouflaged with leaves and flowers to resemble a bower.

The Elders then called for a maiden to sit at the end of the bower as a decoy to lure the beast into the trap but there was not one prepared to risk her life. Repeated appeals went unheard until one of their number suggested that they shave off Owein's beard, attire him in a long, white dress, tinge his lips with the juice of hawthorne berries and place long, golden tresses upon his head. This done, they bound him to a heavy chair and placed him at the far end of the bower where the moonlight would illuminate him. And since he could utter no sound, the river-keeper was unable to warn the *Afanc* that he was a man. At sundown, they waited silently in the copse with strong men ready by the ropes.

At midnight, the *Afanc* emerged from the pool and entered the bower, its silvery voice carrying eerily on the night air. As soon as it was upon the sledge, the men hauled upon the ropes which fell from the overhanging branches across the beast but before they could clamp them to the hoops, a mighty struggle ensued during which the beast clawed out Owein's heart. Yet such was the animosity which the others bore towards him that not a single tear was shed. Even the priest refused him the last rites saying that it was unseemly for these to be administered to one who consorted with witches and was thus a servant of the Devil.

At dawn, two gigantic oxen were hitched to the sledge and with every man lending a hand, they dragged their load along the Afon Lledr track to Dolwyddelan where they rested for the night. Next day they struck northwards, ascending the rugged southern slopes of Carnedd Moel Siabod but this proved too great a strain for one of the oxen which collapsed, its head shaking with such violence that one of its eyes fell out. This put the poor animal in such pain that its tears filled a hollow which became known as Pwll Llyard yr Yeh, that is, the Pool of the Ox's Eye, by which name it is still known today.

Eventually they reached the vale of Gwynant but the ascent of Cwm Dyli proved impossible. Undaunted, they swung north along the track which led to the summit of the Llanberis Pass, there spending the night in freezing cold.

On the third day they summoned every able bodied man in the

vicinity and slowly worked their way up the pathway which is now known as the Miner's Track, past Llyn Tegrn to Llyn Llydaw and then ever upwards until they reached Glaslyn itself. Here they released the *Afanc* which slithered into the lake and never troubled the good people of Arfon again.

Myth or legend? Who can tell. But there are many from Caernarfon to Betws-y-Coed who will declare that the *Afanc* still inhabits Glaslyn, and sheep and goats still vanish mysteriously at night. Not only that, but you will find the *Afanc* Pool and the Beaver Bridge clearly shown on present-day maps.

Perhaps the Elders' decision to incarcerate the giant *Afanc* in Glaslyn is the vital clue since this lake is set amid the most important 'resting place' of all, that is, the Snowdon massif itself.

To the Celts, and for many centuries to follow, Snowdon was known as Gwyddfa, meaning a prominent heap of earth. In time, the story arose that it was the tomb of the giant Rhita whereupon it was invested with the more definitive title of Yr Wyddfa, i.e. The Tumulus.

Now Rhita was the mightiest and most infamous giant who had ever lived and his hobby was collecting the beards of those he killed in combat, his victims including more than a score of princes. One of his contemporaries was King Arthur who, by common consent, sported the most magnificent golden beard in the world. And this Rhita coveted, his ambition being to turn it into a collar for his cloak. Thus he issued a challenge to the king but when the adversaries met, Arthur slew the cruel giant whose body was so large that it took the pile of earth, which is now Snowdon, to cover his body.

As was customary in those days, the Cyfarwydd (Story Tellers) saw the possibilities which the 'news' presented and, no doubt having heard of David and Goliath, magnified the encounter out of all proportion until it matched both its Biblical equivalent and the heroic battle poetry of the Iliad.

In turn, this enhanced Arthur's reputation from being merely legendary to mythological with the result that he became the very heart of the 'Glorious and Heroic Age' to which the *Cymry*[14] clung in times of adversity and which gave them the will to withstand the everlasting incursions made by the Viking, Saxon and Norman hordes. And it was this pride in their past which enabled the Princes of *Cymru*[15] to survive and later sire the future Kings and Queens of England who, in turn, became the mainspring which set Britain on the course of creating an Empire upon which the sun never set.

As so often happens in history, it is the little things which foster the ultimate and grandiose results. So remember as you meander along Snowdon's glorious pathways, those who denigrate legends and mythology fail to realize what profound effects these have upon the existence and prosperity of future generations — including ours!

There may have been another perfectly sound reason for the choice of Glaslyn — at least to the early Welsh. Towering above it and under the lee of the eyrie itself is Bwlch y Saethau (Pass of the Arrows).

Legend has it that King Arthur did not die in the terrible battle of Tre Galan there, thus disclaiming that he sailed to the Other World across Llyn Llydaw. Instead, the story goes, he and his surviving knights sought shelter near Llyn Cwm-y-llan which nestles between Craig Ddu and Yr Aran. There they fell asleep exhausted by their efforts and wounds. Many years later a farmer disturbed the King who opened his eyes only to be informed that the time was not yet at hand. So he returned to his well deserved slumbers and his host still sleep there waiting for the call should Britain need to be saved again. Legend it undoubtedly is but the ancients firmly believed that their saviour would be resurrected in the manner of Christ's second coming if they were pressed beyond mortal endurance. It was that belief which 'kept them going'.

It is also not beyond the bounds of possibility that the good people of Conwy considered that should the *Afanc* manage to escape from Glaslyn they could indeed be pressed far beyond human endurance — but with King Arthur and his doughty warriors mere 'slumbering' nearby, such a calamity could safely be left in his capable hands

With the Welsh, you never know!

POSTSCRIPT. Prior to A.D. 400, the name of Arthur (Artuir or Arturius) was unknown. During the 5th century, however, a soldier of this name certainly existed. In all probability he served as an officer in the Roman cavalry where he became skilled in the arts of warfare. Eventually he commanded about 1,000 highly trained troops, defeating the Saxons in 12 battles and despite contemporary reports being exaggerated, to the Welsh, Arthur became a legendary adjunct to their history.

Now the *Cwmry* take great pride in the authenticity of their heritage. Hence, it is unwise to quote from Sir Arthur Mallory's *Morte d'Arthur* in their presence, for he gleaned many of his tales from the French who had listened entranced in bygone years as itinerant Welsh bards blatantly distorted fact to elevate Arthur to almost God-like stature. Hence Mallory's stories are no more than travesties.

Neither should Tennyson's Arthurian poetry — 'Idylls of the King' — be cited since they are less credible still and vie with Wordsworth's odes and sonnets celebrating Wellington's victory at Waterloo as being the worst and most inaccurate 'Battle Poetry' in English literature.

By A.D. 600, at least 4 royal families named their sons Arthur.

Craig yr Ysfa

RODERICK OF ANGLESEA

including the old Irish tale concerning
'The Mysterious Ty Helenion and Prince Riryd'

(A.D. 1169)

The feast ended. At a signal from the host, Gwyn Felyn[1] rose and the guests settled down to enjoy an evening of story-telling.

'Prince Roderick of Anglesea, son of Owain Gwynedd and unmatched philosopher in the realms of logic, fathered many princes, their names being. . .'

As was the custom on such occasions, a bard's oration began with a eulogy proclaiming his patron's legendary virility, and though no mention was made of any daughters, the audience assumed the existence of these relatively unimportant creatures who attracted little sympathy and less affection. Likewise, diplomatic omissions were made regarding siblings sired during chance encounters, their origins and identities being best ignored if not entirely forgotten.

And this story concerns three of those whose names went unheralded.

Prince Roderick was handsome, brave and possessed of a wisdom far beyond his years. So it was hardly surprising that he was constantly pursued by a retinue of tall, golden-haired Celtic beauties who made no secret of their matrimonial aspirations. Despite their amorous advances, Roderick lost his heart to a demure and deeply religious maiden of fifteen summers whom he quickly took as his wife.

Their union proved to be a happy one for his young bride was of a most affectionate nature and gloried in the joys of motherhood. Over the next ten years, Gwenllian[2] presented him with ten sons in whose upbringing she was eventually assisted by her young niece, Enid, an exceedingly plain and self-effacing girl who Roderick scornfully derided as being totally devoid of any feminine attributes save those of a good education and an aptitude for ministering unto the sick.

While this may well have been true, Enid's disposition was undoubtedly moulded by her mother's death in childbirth and, as a consequence of her father having selflessly insisted on

36

rearing his only child without other assistance, she had been deprived of female insight.

Enid was barely sixteen when her father fell ill. Realizing that his daughter's chances of achieving a good marriage were remote, he arranged for her to be joined in wedlock with a relatively prosperous *uchewyr*[3] named Geraint who dwelled in Deheubarth where he was Bailiff Itinerant of a *Cantref*. Within weeks her father died when, in accordance with his wishes, the nuptial ceremony took place immediately.

Enid was taken aback at the groom's appearance. While obviously of gentle disposition and fine manners, he was slight of build, short in stature, walked with a pronounced limp and the pallor of his face revealed that he was not the most robust of men. And though he was hardly the acme of any maiden's desires, she comforted herself that she would be the mistress of a splendid wooden house and free from Roderick's constant jibes.

Nor were her initial fears unfounded for while the union was consummated and her husband proved to be the kindliest of men, thereafter she endured a virtually companionate and childless marriage. A year later, Geraint was stricken by a strange malady, his cheeks turning sallow and all strength departed from his body, this forcing him to relinquish his post and take to his bed. In the years which followed, Enid nursed him devotedly, taking charge of his affairs and superintending the staff which gradually decreased as their fortune ebbed away.

After four years of matrimony, Geraint breathed his last, leaving Enid with little but a house she was unable to maintain and a letter advising her to return to Gwynedd and seek shelter with her aunt. With no alternative, she swallowed her pride, attired herself in her finest raiment and set out for Anglesea determined that never again would she be thrust into marriage with an unknown suitor, or endure poverty. In Deheubarth she had noted how such ignominies were avoided. It was not difficult for a desirable woman to have men dancing upon her attendance and also be richly rewarded for her favours.

Those four years had hardly been the happiest in Roderick's life either. With Gwenllian doting upon her children whom she steadfastly refused to foster out, he found that she was devoting an increasing measure of her time and energy to being a mother, with a corresponding decrease in her ardour as a lover. Eventually, he came to feel unwanted, even unnecessary to the marriage and, for the first time, the blandishments of maidens whom he met during the course of his official duties began to attract him like a lodestone.

One day, after returning from Bangor, he found Gwenllian conversing animatedly with a companion. She was a young woman of exquisite beauty, swathed in a long, white dress, tightly gathered at the waist to accentuate the full endowment which nature had bestowed upon her lithe and supple body. She rose in deference to his rank, her slender pale hands weaving a delicate tracery through the air. As he strode across the bower, a gasp of admiration left her lips and the gorse-hued tresses which cascaded from her head fell back revealing her high cheek bones and miniature gold pendants tumbling from small, translucent ears.

Roderick regarded her intently. Despite her enchanting appearance, there was something indefinable about her presence which roused memories of the past.

'Fair lady!' he greeted her, acutely aware that his heart was pounding with unaccustomed speed and his breath had shortened. 'Pray make thy identity known unto me.'

Her smile was like a sunburst. 'Noble prince! I am but a poor widow, oft scorned as being devoid of all feminine attributes.' She paused and pursed her lips, almost invitingly. 'My name is equally simple being . . .'

That voice! It was more exciting and melodic than Roderick had ever heard before — as though a heavenly harp was softly resounding in its highest octave.

'. . Enid!'

The single word reverberated through his brain like a bowstring unleashed leaving him bereft of speech. Her soft lips parted slowly and her eyes revealed, unmistakably, a recognition of the devastating effect she had wrought upon him. As from afar he heard Gwenllian's voice.

'Poor Enid has been left in penury,' his wife informed him. 'She begs thee grant her sanctuary, offering to serve as a handmaiden in return.'

Enid's soft eyes beseeched him imploringly. He forced himself to rein his galloping turn of mind. 'Nay! That I will not permit,' he ordained. 'It is not fitting for a relative of thine to be treated as an abigail and quartered with the bondwomen. Would it not be more expedient for thee to take Enid as a lady's companion thus bringing thee company during my absences and thereby raise her estate?'

He turned to Enid: 'By my faith! I treated thee most discourteously in the past but now I pledge to make amends for that injury. And while I would willingly take thee into my household, there are those who may consider thy presence here unseemly.

'What say thee, Gwenllian, if we lodge thy niece in the *ty*[4] at present occupied by the Steward of Llangefni, granting him in lieu the tenancy of the South Aelwyn *hafod*, that being even more convenient for his duties?'

'So be it, my lord,' Gwenllian replied gratefully.

Seven days later, Roderick conducted Enid to her new home. She marvelled at the opulent furnishings which graced every room: the oaken table and carved chairs replete with soft cushions; the woven curtains hanging at every horn-screened window; and sweet smelling rushes covering the floor. While in the bedchamber stood a huge, elegantly canopied divan whose figured cordwain drapes were drawn back to reveal a deeply luxurious mattress, coverlets of the softest lambswool and a quilt of embroidered silk — a boudoir fit for a queen, she thought, or mayhap, a prince's *cariad*![5]

'Shouldst thou desire ought else for thy comfort,' Roderick let fall, 'pray make thy wishes known to me for while thou art under my protection, there is nothing thou shalt lack.'

'God prosper thee!' she blessed. 'After the suffering I have endured these long years, I know not in what manner I can repay thy bounty.'

'Was thy husband a mean and cruel man?' he asked.

'Nay! Mean and cruel he knowingly was not but neither was he a man. I gave him the best four years of my life but I have more fingers on my hands than the nights during which he had to do with me. For the past three years I have been as a nun. Now, for my pains, I am widowed, childless and past the age when men will look upon me favourably.'

'That is not so! 'Tis the contrary which be true. Thou hast blossomed into a flower beyond compare and I swear that there is not one man in the whole of Gwynedd who would not take thee unto himself most willingly.'

'Good sire! Pander not to my misfortunes. How can a prince set apart from others know how they think or feel?'

'Fairest Enid! That I know full well for neath these trappings of rank lies a man whose heart and dreams differ little from those of others.'

She regarded him intently. 'My lord! While thy mastery of logic is renowned, the rudiments of reasoning I learned from my father lead me to challenge your argument.' Her voice took on a coquettish note: 'Pray inform me, sire, since thou holdest that there is not a man in Gwynedd who would not take me unto him most willingly and, when unadorned, a prince and mere mortals are but the same, doth this not infer — at least in logic — that a prince would do likewise?'

'Since I was joined in wedlock,' Roderick replied, 'I have not been with any woman save my wife. Yet this was not because of logic for that smooth-tongued imposter does not concern itself with affairs of the heart or human desires. Once I shared a love which knew no bounds but now Gwenllian is so consumed by the needs of her children that she is heedless to mine, forever asleep when I enter the bedchamber — fatigued by her efforts on behalf of others. Thus I fear that her love for me hath withered and died.

'Like thee with thy husband, I am now but as a brother to her as you were as a sister to him, lying disconsolately abed, craving for affection and yearning for the immeasurable joy of holding a lover in my arms and feeling her soft caress upon my brow. As the chill dawn redeems me from oblivion, I find my bed is colder still for she has already departed to console those she will not leave to the attentions of a nursemaid. Proud Prince I may be but, unlike the poets, I cannot live by brave words alone. I am a man who needs a woman by his side with whom to share the fount of love which rises within me eternally, returning my fervour as equally as I bestow it.

'Once, when you were but a child, timid and scant of appearance, I spoke of thee in words of cruel arrogance. Now I would repent my transgressions as though before a priest, confessing likewise that I am filled with a yearning for thee which overflows from my heart and mind, rendering sleep impossible. Yet this love is of such great import that I could not bring myself to caress even thy silken cheek except thou shouldst come to me of thine own free will and not out of gratitude. Thus, fear not, dearest Enid, and if my words have offended you, pour not scorn upon me as I did upon you but consider them as a penance and keep them secret as though this was the confessional itself.'

'Oh, Roderick!' Enid returned. 'As a child, I fell in love with thee greatly, marrying only to distance myself from your presence, believing that my feelings could never be requited. That love has never waned and through those lonely nights I spent in Deheubarth, it was for thee I wept, not for him.'

Henceforth, there was seldom a day when Roderick and Enid did not savour the delights of each other's nearness, yet their assignations and demeanour were conducted with such prudence that the world knew not of their passion.

As summer waned, Gwenllian waxed morose; frequent pains seared through her head, a constant nausea clutched at her vitals and a strange lassitude assailed her. During the winter, an increasing pallor stole over her once roseate cheeks and her body became no more than a shadow of its former comliness. And by spring, with all strength departed, she took to her bed.

At this, Enid addressed Roderick: 'I fear that Gwenllian is wasting away. She eats but little, converses seldomly and shows no interest in the children.'

'That I know,' he replied, 'except during the pitch of night when she tosses and turns abed, her brow feverish as she speaks in a demented tongue which is foreign to me. Do what you can for her and the children to ease their anguish.'

'That I shall do willingly . . . though this cannot be for long since I am now with child.'

'God in Heaven, woman! Why has thou permitted this to come about?'

'Why didst thou, my love?' she countered quietly. 'When a woman is her master's mistress she does not command her own fate. Couldst not thou have controlled thy passion the better until after Gwenllian's. .?'

The unspoken word paralysed Roderick's nimble tongue. The advent of fatherhood and the possibility that Gwenllion may die were not prospects which had previously crossed his mind. As they did, a train of suspicious thought, bereft of all reason, swirled incoherently round his brain.

'As thy belly swells gross, the finger of calumny will point at me,' he informed Enid. 'Thus thou must depart this place and take refuge with my brother Riryd in Ireland until the child is born so avoiding scurrilous gossip.'

'Cast me not thither,' she pleaded, 'for I cannot face life without thee, yet have Gwenllian face death without serving her until the end.'

Until the end! Roderick's erstwhile suspicions took root as an indictment — that Enid's insistence upon remaining with his wife was little less than prime evidence that she was slowly poisining her victim to speed her own ambitions. Yet proof there was none, nor would such ever be revealed.

'Nay! That cannot be!' he commanded. 'There are those who, in the past, I have chastized for indolence and dishonesty. If your condition were to become known unto them, they would seek to settle old scores, whispering that I had rid myself of my consort to take another. Nothing must prevail which may disrupt the present unity of Wales. Hence thou wilt go thither either of thine own free will or be carried there forcibly.'

Following Enid's departure, Roderick called upon three nuns to succour Gwenllian whose condition at once began to improve.

Seven months later, when she was fully recovered, news arrived that Enid had died bringing forth a son whom his brother had named Enion and pledged to foster. And while the prince informed his wife of her niece's death, the child's parentage he kept privy unto himself.

'Is thy heart broken now that Enid has passed on?' Gwenllian queried when she heard the news.

Roderick remained silent.

'Reproach not thyself,' she continued. 'From the start I saw that she had caught thee in a web as would a spider. Yet I could not bring myself to censure either of you for the blame rests with me alone.'

'That I cannot understand,' Roderick replied hesitantly.

'For too long I gave all my time to the children, disregarding he who fathered them. Had I but given half my love to thee, then thou wouldst not have been driven into the arms of another. I prayed constantly for God's forgiveness and intercession but He harkened not. And this I took as my punishment for not harkening unto thee. As time went by, my guilt bored into my soul as doth a worm into a sheep's entrails until I lost the will to live. At last a ray of hope shone from the heavens. You despatched her from your side, though for what reason I knew not. And, with her departure, the worm likewise took leave of me and life returned.'

'Oh, Gwenllian! Proud prince though thy husband may be, yet he has also been the greatest of fools. True, ignored and unloved did I feel and sought affection elsewhere until I perceived that this was but an artifice to gain power. That which crucified thee was not God's punishment. Rather would I believe that she was administering slow poison unto thee. Thus I sent her packing whereupon God inflicted His wrath upon her.'

'Is that what you truly believe, Roderick?'

'Aye! Though this I can never prove. If only I had the power to turn back the calendar. . .'

'In that I would gladly assist thee, obliterating all which hath come to pass these three score moons and lay with thee once more as thy wife.'

That night, Roderick and Gwenllian found a love greater than they had ever known before and their union was soon doubly blessed by twin girls whom he came to love dearly.

Helen and Angharad were as indistinguishable as they were inseparable. All they possessed they shared equally and everything they did was together, neither were there any rivalries nor jealousies, their trust in each other being complete. Soon the girls became aware that every thought was known unto the other without a word being spoken so that there was never a secret between them. Indeed, the only distinction betwixt them was that Helen was passionately fond of dogs, she being devoted to her black hunting hound, while Angharad was indifferent to their existence.

As they reached maidenhood their beauty was famed and there were many who sought their hands in marriage. This, however, was not an estate that appealed to them for the thought of separation was unendurable. When they reached their eighteenth year, Roderick, in desperation, spoke with Cadell ap Owain, a kinsman of Rhys ap Tewdwr, Prince of Deheubarth, who had two sons, Iago who was 14, and Rhys aged 16, proposing that a dual union would further strengthen the bonds which existed between the two principalities.

When the two families met, the two young men could hardly believe their good fortune in being matched with such striking beauties. And with the sisters being identical, neither was concerned as to which maiden he wed, being content to leave the choice to them.

Helen and Angharad, however, were greatly apprehensive, for being in the full bloom of womanhood, they regarded their suitors as no more than inexperienced striplings rather than men in the image of their beloved father. Since there was no better prospect in sight, and this arrangement did, at least, ensure that they remained together, they agreed to the unions albeit that neither of the young men attracted either maiden sufficiently to choose between them. And while they both agreed that by virtue of his age, Rhys should be the better lover, they decided to draw lots, whereupon Helen acquired Rhys while Angharad found herself saddled with the fourteen-year-old Iago. With the dilemma thus resolved, the nuptial ceremony was set to coincide with the Feast of Fertility on the 1st May.

Early in November, a young man of magnificent appearance arrived at Roderick's *llys*[6] bearing a sealed letter from Ireland. This revealed that the bearer was no other than Enion whom Riryd commended for high office. Roderick was instantly impressed by his son's scholarship which encompassed latin, history, theology, mathematics, logic and poetry, together with a fine knowledge of equitation, hunting and the tactics of warfare. And such was Enion's commanding presence that his father appointed him Comptroller of Pleas, Fines, Redemptions and Ransoms, lodging him in the house wherein his mother once abode.

Enion's arrival did not pass unnoticed by the maidens of
Anglesea who, despite pursuing him with single-minded intent,
found him indifferent to their charms. All, that is, save one.

Helen and Angharad met Enion daily and soon a close friendship
developed between the three of them. It was Enion who accompanied them while riding; it was Enion who made them laugh; and
Enion to whom they confided their anxieties concerning the
forthcoming nuptials, so that he became more of a wise and elder
brother to them than those of their own flesh and blood.

One evening, Roderick despatched Helen to Enion's house with
a list of pleas for consideration. It was the first time that either of
the maidens had been alone with him and whereas conversation
came easily when the three were together, he now appeared ner-
vous. She looked up at him and caught his eye. At once the entire
room dissolved and all she saw was Enion standing before her. A
tremor passed through her body, followed by another and yet
another until her breath shortened and she saw Enion trembling,
too. He strode quickly towards her.

'Oh, fairest Helen! Since I first saw you I have not known a
moment's peace. By day, I see your face constantly before me,
while at night the sweet smell of your hair intoxicates me so that,
in my slumbers, I feel you lying tenderly in my arms. My love for
you is such that I cannot bear to go through life without you by
my side. Forswear Rhys and, by my faith, you shall never fear the
marriage bed again.'

She felt his arms encompass her powerfully and his lips consume
her own until she was aware of nought but the pounding of his
heart against her breast and the burning love for him within her
soul.

Later, as she returned to her father's house, Helen became fearful
that Angharad would instinctively divine her secret but when they
met, her sister made no sign of discernment. That night she lay
awake, burdened by the dread of her father's anger when she
disclosed her desires: and guilty that her feelings for Enion exceeded
the love which she bore towards Angharad and would thus tear
them apart.

Three days later Angharad entered their bedchamber. 'Helen!'
she whispered. 'I beg thee not to hate me but I cannot wed Iago.
Yet I am tortured by the fear of our father's wrath when he hears
of this.'

'Then I shall help thee,' Helen replied, 'saying that I, too, am
unable to face lying abed with a boy and would rather remain an
eternal maiden than suffer usage of this nature.'

'Would that thy sacrifice be of avail,' Angharad returned, 'but that it will not be for I have at once both a heaviness and joy in my heart. My sorrow is that this very joy means more to me than thou dost for I have lost my heart to another and would follow him to the last ends of the earth. I beg of thee, be not too angered with me.'

'That I am not,' Helen answered, 'for thy happiness is mine also.'

'Sweet Helen! For that, I love thee more greatly than ever. But will our father understand when I say that I knew nothing of this myself until a short hour ago. I did not realize how feelings could change with such haste. Canst thou believe this, Helen? Of all men, it is Enion?'

Early next morning Helen disclosed her love for Enion to her mother.

'The anguish of love is an affliction concerning which I know full well,' Gwenllian assured her. 'It blinds one's eye to reality, destroys reason and transcends all other attachments. Accordingly, I will speak with thy father for beneath his stern approach there lies a heart not indifferent to affection. Doth Angharad know of Enion's desire to wed thee?'

'Nay! Tis privy to the three of us.'

Later that day, Angharad came unto her mother saying: 'Lo! I cannot wed Iago for my heart lies with Enion. Pray speak with my father on my behalf.'

'Does Enion requite thy love?'

'That I know not for as yet I have made no declaration unto him.'

'Does Helen know of this?'

'That she does.'

'Then say no more to any other and I will speak to thy father.'

At this, Gwenllian hastened to her husband. On hearing of the vexatious triangle he sank into his chair, head bowed and cupped in his hands. 'Oh, my God! The mill-stone hath ground its full circle. Is the House of Gwynedd to be forever cursed with sorrow?'

'That I know not but we may yet limit the grasp of its visitation. Should our daughters be forced into marriage with Rhys and Iago, I warrant that none of them will reap one ear of happiness. Inevitably, wild oats will be sewn. Nor will Enion harvest anything but sorrow. If, however, Helen be wedded unto her heart's desire, though this may turn Angharad against us all, the wretchedness will be confined to one. What sayest to that, Roderick?'

'That I forbid! Wouldst thou have me violate my pledge to Cadell and sow distrust between the two principalities?'

'Is thy pride greater than the happiness of others?' his wife countered. 'I prithee, destroy not heart's fond favour. Love turns reason asunder, changes darkness into light and hopelessness into life eternal. That we both know well. Surely Cadell will understand after his own tribulation. Or can there be some reason stronger than love itself which commands thy heart to deny it to others?'

'Nay, Gwenllian, there is not! But there is one love which divorces reason from my head, understanding from my heart and silences my tongue.'

'Hast thou spoken with thy priest concerning this?'

'That I have not! What doth a wifeless priest know of human love? The confessional concerns itself only with sin and the penance thereof. Nor doth the church itself brook tolerance in the enforcement of its own creed of justice.'

'Oh, Roderick! If you cannot put your trust in those who claim to be the servants of God, can you not confide your anguish in one who loves you more than life itself? Or hast thou a secret too grave for even I to countenance?'

'My love! Nineteen years ago my shame and fears overcame honour and honesty. I should have confessed then as I ought to have done when Enion arrived. . . Would you have your daughter wed a half-brother?'

'Is that all which troubles you?' Gwenllian soothed. 'Though I admit to once wondering if you were verily the father of Enid's child, upon reflection I knew this could never be. During the long years she dwelled in Deheubarth, despite my gross insensibility to thy advances, thou hadst to do with me not infrequently, yet nothing came of these encounters, nor after Helen and Angharad were born.'

'Then how dost thou account for them?' Roderick enquired.

'Their conception was an Act of God wherein he showed his forgiveness to both of us.'

'But what of Enion's genesis?'

'If, as thou hast said, Enid was prepared to administer poison and thus take the life of one who stood in the way of her ambitions, when she found that her union with thee was not fruitful, is it beyond reason to suspect that she was not equally capable of furthering her advancement by creating life in the form of another's child and then holding thee accountable. Alas! That we shall never know for only the mother can gainsay the parentage of the child she bears.'

'Oh, Gwenllian! Though Plato himself could not dismiss thy logic, should either of us have been lax in our presumptions, we consign Enion to the most shameful bastardy of all and that I cannot bring myself to prescribe.

'Yet, how can I confide my lechery to others? Since the bastard Cynan seized the throne of Gwynedd, this House has been plagued by illegitimacy. Even my own father has sired more siblings out of wedlock than there are swordsmen and archers in his *teulu*.[7] Since my own fall from faithfulness I have striven to redeem that trespass by preaching chastity to my followers. Should the truth be revealed, the sharpened finger of hypocrisy would point at my heart and my word become no more than a mockery.

'For all his faults, my father has bonded the peoples of Wales into a nation capable of withstanding King Henry. But now my father's years are numbered. And though Dafydd and Hywell will succeed him as joint rulers, if my repute be tarnished, what voice shall I have to mediate should discord arise between them — as it surely will? Thus, is Enion to be crucified upon the cross of Wales? Or should I risk my grandchildren being born with addled wits?'

For Roderick, the night was long and sleepless, his mind torn between the conflicting allegiances of family and state. Nor did the cold December morn which followed cool his fevered mind.

Towards mid-day, his brother Dafydd arrived in great haste saying unto him: 'Lo! As thou well knowest, our father has ordained that upon his death, Hywell and I should rule Gwynedd jointly. Yet I fear that his mind must have been afflicted by the ravages of dotage when he made that decree for my brother is but a weakling poet unfit to defend this fair land. He is, however, over-ambitious and now gathers his followers about him to seize the throne when our illustrious father breathes his last. Wilt thou pledge thyself unto me against the usurper?'

'Dafydd! Thou, too, art greatly ambitious, though I fear this to be for thyself rather than for Wales. Would it not be better for our country if both you and Hywell sacrificed personal appetites and threw your lots behind Iorwerth whom the Elders will rightly see as the most notable amongst us?'

'That I will never concede,' Dafydd sneered. 'The bards have always held that only God can take away the rights of the eldest son. Thus I am the rightful heir. Sacrifice what you choose but seek not to subvert others to thy buckled sense of righteousness.'

'Then I shall pray that our father outlives the pair of thee,' Roderick retorted.

'Go thee then, brother! Waste thy time closeted in prayer as Hywell does composing foolish verse while I work towards Gwynedd's salvation.'

Dafydd's words rung within Roderick's mind: 'Sacrifice what you choose but seek not to subvert others. . .' By eventide, he

came to a decision whereupon he spoke to Enion, revealing to him
not only his parentage but all that preceding it, together with the
remorse and dangers which ensued. 'There are those who seek to
tear Gwynedd asunder and with it, all Wales,' he concluded. 'If this
sorry tale be advertised, there are many who would use it to
discredit the House of Gwynedd itself. Should this come to pass,
the English hordes will devour Arfon piecemeal and we shall
become as bondmen unto them, employed as oxherds, fowlers and
tillers of the land. Wouldst thou have that upon thy conscience?'

Enion's eyes blazed. 'Would you had a conscience such as this
before fornicating with your wife's kinswoman,' he rasped. 'Is it
not thee who, by thy lust, has put Wales at risk? Yea, you who
bestowed upon my mother rubies, amethysts, golden beads and
necklaces in payment for the usage of her body to satiate thy carnal
lust! I warrant you were not thinking of Gwynedd upon the night
you spawned me, nor yet when you banished my mother to
Ireland, leaving her to die in sin as she brought forth a bastard son
whose advent you have kept secret these nineteen years! You speak
to me of slavery! But have you not consigned my very heart unto
an equal bondage serving me no better than those who dwell to the
east of Offa's Dyke?'

Roderick recoiled from Enion's attack to which he knew there
was no defence. He saw the passion recede from his son's face and
the cold steel of enmity flash within his eyes.

'Art thou prepared to duel with me?' Enion challenged.

'Nay! I have harmed thee too greatly already. I will not raise
sword against you even if I be charged with cowardice.'

'I speak not of swordsmanship but of a greater weapon regarding
which you profess to be supreme. Art thou not Prince of Anglesea
by birth and unmatched philosopher by repute?'

'That is so!'

'Then I will duel with you in the realm of which you are the pro-
fessed master. But first I would prepare my proposition. Thus, on
the seventh day hence, I will speak to you again. Until then you
can place thy trust in me. Not being partial to incest I shall not seek
to lure or abduct Helen from thy presence.'

Thus it was with many misgivings that, on the following morning, the prince set out for Bangor where the Court of Elders was
in session. He was still smarting from the arrows of home-truth
which Enion had fired in his direction: nor was the young man's
pledge of honourable intent sufficient to dispel the spectre of
mistrust which haunted his troubled mind.

Upon Roderick's departure, Enion conferred with Gwenllian

who drew aside the veil which concealed many mysteries. Later he spoke with Helen who declared that her love for him transcended all that she bore unto her parents or Angharad whom she now mistrusted.

On the morrow, Enion made his way to the Brook of the Beavers[8] from whence he ascended to Twll Du where he confided his predicament to Mhaira.

'The Isle of Môn is indeed a troubled realm', she replied. 'Already I have been approached by Angharad who begged me to prepare a potion to give unto thee so that thou wouldst requite her love and remain faithful to her for life. Could it be that thou art seeking a similar preparation to aid thy cause?'

'Nay! I am not a fool. Magic of that degree does not exist. It is the wisdom of the Druids for which I crave. The psalms proclaim that I was shapen in Iniquity and in sin did my mother conceive me. Tell me, oh wise one, are the sins of the fathers visited upon their children, yea, unto the third generation?'

'That they are not! This is no more than another delusion in Christian mythology. Our ancient philosophy holds that it is the traits which are passed on, our very existence being no more than Nature's way of preserving these traits for ever.

'Thy problem lies not with sin but is governed by ancestry. I have frequently observed Prince Roderick and his father but neither in countenance, build nor disposition dost thou appear to have inherited a single one of their traits. Only a child's mother can confirm its paternity but, alas, her witness now lies interred with her poor bones. Hence proof is not accessible unto thee. Yet there is another way by which Prince Roderick's logic may be confounded and, albeit this may destroy him, I will reveal it unto thee most willingly. . .'

On the seventh day Enion addressed himself to Roderick: 'Before commencing my discourse, I relinquish my post as Comptroller and thus being no longer in thy employ, I can speak freely, though I pity those who enter their pleas before thee and must endure thy own notion of justice. In thy absence have I betrayed thy trust, great prince?'

'That you have not.'

'Then have I still thy trust?'

'That is so.'

'Then, in logic, thou art a fool,' Enion began, 'for who is there who owes thee trust in return? Dost thou trust thy brothers, Dafydd and Hywell, who would tear Gwynedd asunder with their covetous ambition?'

'What knowest thou of that?'

'No less than thyself! Dost thou trust Helen and Angharad whom you seek to force into marriages they both renounce? Or thy mistress whom thou monstrously despatched to another land when the profit of thy lust became an embarrassment to thee? And then compounded this felony by instantly returning to thy wife's bed! And when she became full with child, were you so foolish as to believe that my mother would not hear of this, and like any woman so grievously scorned, would not seek retribution even from her grave? And finally, proud Prince, having treacherously deceived your wife, why should you believe that she was incapable of acting in a like manner? Is that thy logic?'

'Defame Gwenllian at thy peril!' Roderick retorted angrily. 'And as for logic, thy case is but a sack of infamous riddles. Is that all you have to offer?'

'Nay, it is not!' Enion replied. 'Pray tell me, before my birth, how many years elapsed since you sired a child?'

'Nigh on five.'

'And since the birth of Helen and Angharad, how many other siblings have you fathered?'

'None.'

'Does your bard still proclaim your virility when only twice in twenty-six years have your loins been fruitful?' Enion let fall. '. . . Or believe that you were!'

'What do you imply by that?' Roderick snapped.

'When my mother passed on she bequeathed unto me not only a prince's ransom in jewels and gold which you showered upon her but also a Last Testament wherein she recorded her crucifixion at the hands of a tyrant no more merciful than Herod himself. Oh, I admit that thy courtesan she became but the very genesis of her fall from virtue lay in the manner you decried her image as a child. Until she fled from your abuse, suffering marriage to a stranger rather than endure the barbs of thy bitter tongue!

Then, when widowhood and privation forced her to seek sanctuary here, your welcoming words, though sweetly honeyed, did not conceal that in return for your benevolence you sought a tariff only a woman could discharge. Thus entrapped by dire necessity she became set upon retribution for thy past scorn.

'But later, amid the pitch of night as you lay sleeping in her arms, too often did she hear you cry out as in prayer for the restoration of your power to beget a child. At that, her heart bled for thee, turning from contempt to love, so that with thy continued failure to accomplish this need, she vowed to restore thy self-esteem no matter what the cost to her may be. That was the true measure of her love.

'Despite thy vile accusations, my mother did not contribute to her aunt's indisposition. That was born of a heart broken by thy heedless betrayal. Had you but known it, you were blessed by the consummate love of two women to which self-pity blinded your eyes. The only venom administered was that which poisoned your heart!'

'How dost thou come to speak of poison?' Roderick demanded.

'Because I know of all things,' Enion responded. 'I was with Taliesin in Bethlehem when Christ was born and at Golgotha as He hung upon the Cross. I was with King Arthur at Baden when he killed 960 of the enemy single-handed. I witnessed his funeral barge sail upon Llyn Llydaw to the Other World. Thus how can I be thy son?

'Apply thy logic to this also. If you hold that neither Gwenllian nor thyself can disprove that I am your son, why did she not oppose my union with Helen but, instead, favour it greatly? Surely thy wife does not sanction incest? Hence there must be a good reason unknown to thee why she is so disposed.

'So whom can you really trust? She whom you have betrayed within the very bounds of thy estate. Apply thy fine logic to that, proud prince! And in so doing, ask thyself a further question, to wit, upon thy return to Gwenllian's bed, didst thou again cry out in thy sleep for the power to fulfil thy aspirations? And did your wife, like my mother, take compassion upon thy sterility and likewise vow to revive thy vanity counting not the cost? Thus, are Helen and Angharad truly the fruit of thy loins or the harvest of a sacrifice to cloak your own deficiency? Unmatched philosopher of logic, ponder these questions!'

'If thou wert not my guest I would kill thee for thy disparagement!' Roderick thundered.

'Ah! That is the historic solution of problems by the House of Gwynedd,' Enion scoffed, 'and it would dispose equally of the question of marriage. But would it stay the doubts now rampant in thy mind? Nay, only the proven truth can still their racking gripe.'

'The proven truth!' Roderick sneered. 'Thy words are no more than idle speculation, nor hast thou presented a single enlightenment worthy of inquiry. So where lies the truth?'

'It lies where cowards fear to tread!'

'Art thou accusing me of cowardice?' Roderick stormed.

'Nay! Unless thou hast not the courage to tread the pathway to truth.'

'That a prince of Gwynedd always possesses.'

'Then hasten to Gwenllian, informing her that thou art not set upon indictment nor seeking evidence of adultery but only to ascertain whether she indeed found thee sterile and begat thy daughters by another in an unmatched love to conceal thy inadequacy and thus preserve thy self-esteem. Likewise swearing that if this be the truth you shall kneel at her feet in tribute to a love greater than the world has known before save once.'

'That I cannot ask,' Roderick replied. 'I have shamed Gwenllian once and cannot compound this by accusing her of unfaithfulness. That is the measure of my love. As for my wife, if she were to have done as you accuse, this she would never admit for fear of destroying that which infidelity sought to preserve. That is the measure of her love for me!'

'Then you admit that you cannot trust the word of the one whom you profess to love greater than all others?' Enion thrust back. 'That being so, wilt thou now inform thy wife that I am not your son.'

'Without proof that I cannot hold. Wouldst thou have me openly defame thy mother merely to achieve your own object?'

'That is not logic! Thou art merely hiding behind any excuse thou canst conjure up. If you think that I am your son, hold this opinion closely for in seeking to preserve thy false pride, thou art bringing unhappiness to others. Thus you cannot have fathered me. Accordingly, I shall now depart to an island greater than thine.'

With Roderick's trust in Enion being totally destroyed, he charged his *teulu* to mount watch over him. On the third day their leader reported that he had set sail for Ireland whereupon the prince commanded his followers to prepare for his daughters' marriages with all speed, a decision which attracted no opposition from either his wife or the maidens themselves. Helen's quiet acquiescence not only perplexed her father but sowed the seeds of suspicion in his mind whereupon he bade Angharad not to let her sister out of her sight perchance she attempted to follow Enion to Ireland.

On the seventh morning Angharad came unto her father saying: 'Lo! When I awoke I found that Helen was gone.'

'Did I not give orders for the door to be locked?' Roderick roared.

'That it still was but the window was cut open.'

'Art thou saying that you did not hear the uproar this must have occasioned?'

'That I did not but my mind is so benumbed I fear I was drugged into unconsciousness,' his daughter replied.

A search was immediately mounted but all it revealed was that Helen's old, pet dog was also missing. Fleet horsemen were at once despatched to all ports but it was late afternoon before the news was received from Moel-y-don that a small vessel which arrived from Port Dyn Norwig[9] on the previous evening had set sail at dawn towards whence it came carrying two passengers and a large black hound. Thus it was not until the following morning that Roderick was able to reassemble his *teulu* at Caernarfon.

At first light, horsemen scoured all roads to the northern and westerly ports while others covered the tracks leading to Dol Badarn and Llyn Cwellyn. Around noon-tide, a violent storm arose blanketing the entire principality with a deep layer of snow, this continuing for two days forcing men and beast alike to seek shelter.

On the third day the elements relented and it was established that the travellers had been seen in the vicinity of Rhaeadr Ogwen. Horsemen were despatched to Capel Curig and the head of Nant Ffrancon to isolate the fugitives. Both bands struggled to within a mile of their quarry when Enion espied them.

'To the ridge!' Helen commanded. 'The horses cannot follow us there.'

'We shall die up there at night,' Enion warned.

'I would sooner freeze to death quickly,' Helen replied, 'rather than face life without thee — for thou wilt die most cruelly should my father lay hands on thee.'

With that, Enion led Helen through the deep drifts by Afon Llugwy towards the mountain fastness. One group of soldiers moved after them while a second headed towards the Ysgolion Duon escarpment where the going was easier. Dusk was already descending when the lovers reached the crags. There, on finding their adversaries approaching from the west, they began to scramble eastwards up the narrow, ice-encrusted ridge which soared high above the precipitous chasm of Cwm Eigiau, twelve hundred feet below. Almost at once a howling gale drove a curtain of snow and stinging ice before it blinding the pursuers who, fearful for their lives, descended to Ffynnon Llugwy.

Next morning they tried again but all they found was the lifeless body of Helen's faithful hound upon the summit above the ridge.

Nothing was ever seen or heard of Helen or Enion again except that sometimes, when dusk fell and the wind screamed over the ridge, two spectral figures were seen ascending to the summit which, henceforth, was dubbed Pen yr Helgi-du, that is, The Mountain of the Black Hound: while the ridge itself was christened Craig yr Ysbryd, which means Crag of the Ghosts.

Over the centuries there were many who swore that, even on the
hottest day, those who traversed Craig yr Ysbryd experienced a feeling of cold descend upon them which made every part of their bodies
itch. Hence, Ysbryd became contracted to the name by which it is
known today, Craig yr Ysfa, i.e. The Crag of Feeling or Itching.

But did Helen and Enion really die upon the unforgiving
Carnedds? In Galway, they used to tell of a fine house which a rich
stranger and his wife built overlooking the bay, though not even
the most ancient of the white-beards knew how it acquired its
unusual name of 'Ty Helenion'. Or why their children's God-father
was Prince Riryd!

I think I do. And I hope that I'm right!

True or false? Fact or legend? Well, it is historically proven that
Roderick ap Owain Gwynedd was Prince of Môn and a noted
philosopher. It is equally correct that he fathered and fostered
many sons all of whom were princes, while one of his sons was certainly fostered by his brother Riryd who owned a large estate in
Ireland.

Furthermore, Gwynedd and Deheubarth were traditionally linked
by frequent arranged marriages between their respective rulers'
sons and daughters, and intermarriage in the *uchewyr* class was a
commonplace occurrence.

While a number of somewhat sketchy 'legends' have survived
regarding the alleged manner in which various peaks, crags and
ridges in the Carneddau gained their names, these are often of such
a mystical nature that their origins are obviously the result of bardic influence. Against this, those in Mhaira's Wondertale certainly
bear the ring of feasible truth.

Finally, Roderick was 59 when Helen and Enion eloped in
February 1169, just ten months prior to Owain Gwynedd's death.
From that time henceforth: 'Roderick was as a broken man.' Since
Owain's early demise was more or less anticipated, and the subsequent strife attributable to Dafydd's and Hywell's ambitions clearly
forseen, there must have been another potent cause of Roderick's
distress. And what could have been more likely to have occasioned
this than the belief that he was personally responsible for Helen's
and Enion's deaths?

The evidence rests: I leave the judgement to you.

MHAIRA AND MADOC

The legend which tells how the Black coven of Gwynedd
helped Prince Madoc to discover America.

(*circa* A.D. 1170)

Owain Gwynedd had a son named Madoc who, unlike many of his
brothers, displayed scant regard for the affairs of state or the arts
of warfare. His interest lay in the oceans beyond the scenes of
battle, and within his *cantrefs*, which bordered the coast of the
Principality, he had attracted a large following of sea-faring men
who not only loved him greatly but revered him as a fine poet and
the greatest navigator Gwynedd had ever known.

Shortly after Owain's death, Madoc's brother, Dafydd, came unto him saying: 'Lo! Have not the bards, even since Taliesen,
proclaimed that only God can take away the rights of the eldest
son? Thus, as my father's firstborn, I am the rightful heir to
Gwynedd. Yet our brother, Hywell, opposes my succession. Wilt
thou summon thy followers and join me against the usurper?'

To this Madoc replied: 'In his wisdom, our father ordained that
you and Hywell should rule jointly.'

'That is so,' Dafydd admitted, 'but I fear that our illustrious
father's mind must have been afflicted by the ravages of dotage
when he made that decree. Hywell, though over-ambitious, is but
a weakling caring for nought but the harp, poetry and song. He
doth little but compose verse, oft closeting himself for days on end
whilst contemplating the construction of a single stanza in an effort
to achieve perfect *cynghanedd*[1]. He possesses neither the courage
nor ability to defend Gwynedd against the King of Powys who
would then conquer this fair land and enslave us all.'

'Be that as may,' Madoc answered, 'and while I sympathize with
thee, yet I will not bear arms against a brother. Go thou and make
peace with Hywell and rule jointly.'

Whereupon Dafydd departed in anger.

On the following day, Hywell came unto Madoc saying: 'Lo!
Since the days of the great Cunedda it has been the custom, upon
the death of ruling prince, for the Court of Elders to elect the most
worthy of his sons to succeed him. Now Dafydd seeks to repudiate

tradition by claiming the right of inheritance as the eldest son in the manner of the Saxons. Wilt thou summon thy followers and join me against the usurper?'

To this Madoc replied: 'In his wisdom, our father ordained that you and Dafydd should rule jointly.'

'That is so,' Hywell admitted, 'but I fear that our illustrious father's mind must have been afflicted by the ravages of dotage when he made that decree. Dafydd is over-ambitious, living only by the sword, eschewing the harp, poetry and song. If he were to ascend the throne he would straightway plunge Gwynedd into a cruel war against Powys as the first step in his desire to become Bretwalda of all Wales, thus permitting the King of England to fall upon our left flank and conquer this fair land and enslave us all.'

'Be that as may,' Madoc answered, 'and while I sympathize with thee, yet I will not bear arms against a brother. Go thou and make peace with Dafydd and rule jointly.'

Whereupon Hywell departed in anger.

On the morrow Prince Madoc journeyed to Llyn Ogwen and ascended the stony pathway by the unnamed lake to where the Coven of Twll Du lived.

'Why comest thou to our poor abode, sire?' Mhaira asked of him.

'I have heard fine reports of thy prowess in the realms of philosophy and astronomy,' he replied. 'Thus I come to seek thy counsel.'

'Thou seekest knowledge from a witch?', she returned in amazement.

'I will seek the truth from God or the Devil himself if either knows it,' Madoc went on, 'for I have visited lands where neither of them appear to have trod.'

'And where be that?' Mhaira enquired.

'I have navigated the great oceans to Iceland and beyond, sailing among vast mountains of ice which float upon the sea, one day reaching a country which is known to others as Greenland and where snow abounds eternally. There, in the summer, night doth not exist yet, during the months of winter, it is devoid of day. And those who dwell in these savage regions speak in a strange tongue which falls harshly upon the ear. By chance, I was accompanied by an interpreter of tongues from Iceland and through him I learned of a great island to the west which is perpetually shrouded in mist and where the surrounding seas boil with fine fish[2]. Moreover, they told me of another country, still further distant, of such dimension that no one hath ever voyaged to its extremity and where men hunt strange animals thrice the size of our largest oxen, and till ceaselessly, reaping two harvests each year.

'Concerning this I have spoken with the most learned men in the church who, with one voice, declare that this is no more than a legend concerning the Other World. And should I sail thus far westwards I will surely drop off the edge of the earth and so fall into the bottomless Pit of Acheron.'

'Dost thou believe that which the priests tell thee?'Mhaira countered.

'I know not what to believe!'

'I, too, have heard tell of this Greenland and the Misty Isle to which the Vikings sailed three hundred years ago. Hence I will pose thee a question. If a ship, sailing westwards, can fall off the edge of the world, would not the oceans have already done likewise?'

'That is a reasoning which had not occurred to me,' Madoc admitted. 'Unless, that is, the earth is surrounded by a barrier of high land to retain the waters upon it.'

'That would indeed be necessary if, as you and your priests believe, the earth is flat!'

'How otherwise can it be?'

'Is the moon flat also?'

'I have not been persuaded to the contrary,' Madoc declared.

Mhaira led the prince to the darkest recess of her cave where she lit a candle. 'This should be likened unto the sun,' she told him while cutting a circle of paper. 'And this would represent the moon if it was flat.'

Next she took another piece of paper in which she carved a slit, holding this between the candle and the 'moon', moving the latter in all directions so that the light passed through the aperture and fell upon it producing reflections which varied from a small segment to full illumination.

'Mark thee well,' Mhaira commanded, 'that the line upon the moon dividing light from dark is always in a straight line.'

She then took a bright metal sphere and moved it in a similar fashion. 'Note carefully,' she advised, 'that the division between light and darkness is no longer a straight line but is always curved. Since the moon reflects the light of the sun, doth this not prove that the moon is likewise a sphere?'

Madoc could only agree.

'Thy priests hold that the sun and the planets encircle the earth which their so-called astronomers declare is the centre of the entire universe. Tell me, Madoc, doth the Gwydians[3] and Aranrhod[4] appear in the skies during the entire period of the four seasons?'

'That they do not! One half of the constellations are seen in midsummer, the other half only come into view during the depth of winter.'

'And do they circle the earth?' she probed.

'Nay! We take our bearings of them from the Great North Star.'

Mhaira arranged three spheres in such a manner that both the sun and the moon moved round the earth. 'See, my prince,' she declared, 'if this be the order, how doth the sun's light reach the moon when it is night upon earth?'

'It cannot!' he conceded.

She then placed the spheres with the moon circling the earth but with both travelling round the sun. 'Look! Canst thou now perceive how, with this arrangement, the sun is able to shine upon the moon even at the time when its rays do not fall upon that part of the earth which is shrouded by night?'

'That I do perceive!' Madoc pronounced.

'Thus the philosophy of thy priests is false!' Mhaira declared triumphantly.

'I cannot argue with thee!'

'Aye! Like many other things which they hold to be true! Tell me, when thou art sailing the seas,' Mhaira interrogated, 'and another ship appears, how is it first seen?'

'First its mast, then its hull.'

'If it is seen from the masthead as opposed to the foredeck, what difference is perceived?'

'We can see the other ship at a greater distance.'

'So the higher you climb, the greater is the distance you are able to see?'

'That is so!'

'When you survey a shoreline devoid of undulations, how far canst thou cast thine eye?'

'Seven miles.'

'Hast thou heard of the philosophy of Pythagoras concerning a triangle?' Mhaira asked.

'Aye! The five, four, three measurement which produces a perfect right-angle.'

' 'Tis more than that! If the length of the longest side be multiplied by itself, the answer is equal to the addition of the separate lengths of the other two sides also multiplied by themselves. Thus if a man's eyes at six feet above the ground can see an object of little height seven miles distant, can the look-out upon a thirty foot mast espy the hull of another ship 28 miles distant?'

'That he cannot see!'

'Why not?'

'Because a man's eyes are not strong enough.'

'But when thou dost see it appear, does it not seem as though the ship is climbing a hill with first the mast appearing followed by the hull?'

'Now that you mention this, it does so appear.'

'Come with me, Madoc, to the Hill of the Hawk[5] and from its summit regard well the horizon.'

On the following day they climbed the mountain from Beddkelert. 'There is no limit to a man's vision,' she pointed out, 'otherwise he could not see the moon, the sun, nor the limitless stars in the heavens. If the earth be flat, by virtue of Pythagoras, thou wouldst be able to see to the limits of the world from this place. But this is not possible. As we descend by the southern brow, mark well the limits of the horizon successively to Llangelynin, Blas Mynach[6] and Harlech, all these distances being well known unto us. This will prove to thee that we are not looking at the base of a triangle at all but what is actually the curved surface of the earth!'

As they descended, Madoc made his calculations, his wonder increasing step by step.

'Lo! The earth is not flat, is it, my prince?' she questioned as they reached Aberglaslyn. 'Does this not show equally, as didst my experiment concerning the moon, that the earth is also round?'

'If that be true,' Madoc countered, 'why does not the sea flow away from here unto a lower level as does a mountain stream from its source to the valley below?'

'There is a power of which we know not', Mhaira confided. 'This holds everything in its appointed place, drawing all to the centre of the earth irrespective of its size or weight. That is why, when we drop a large stone and a small pebble to the ground, they arrive at the same time. The Druid philosophers and astronomers, by the use of circles and calendric stones with holes in them which reveal the light of certain stars only on the same day of each year, have proved that we are not the centre of the universe. Some day, we shall also unravel the mystery of the earth's power. One does not need to know the proof of everything one sees. There are some things in which we can only believe. Hast thou seen thy god?'

'No man hath done that.'

'Hast thou seen the Prince of Darkness?'

'No man hath seen him either.'

'Yet thou believest in both.'

'That is so.'

'Then sail, my Prince, not to the Other World but to a new
land as the Vikings have done before thee.'

'When I return I shall indeed announce that the earth is round',
Madoc declared.

'Aye! And be ex-communicated for blasphemy!' Mhaira derided.
'That is what thy false priests will do to thee. But Satan would not
castigate thee for thy learning. Rather would He welcome a man of
enlightenment. That is the difference between thy God and my
Prince.'

Fortified by Mhaira's assurances, Madoc sailed westwards in his
ship, the Gwennan Gorn. Two years later he returned, his crew
sadly depleted since all the unmarried men had chosen to remain
in the land of milk and honey which they had discovered across the
seas, and where they took unto themselves wives and formed a
tribe of their own blood.

Despite this, the priests told Madoc that he had been most fortunate in not sailing further otherwise he would surely have fallen
off the edge of the world. But the reason why he had not done so
he kept privy to himself and Mhaira.

Soon, tales of the 'promised land' spread throughout Madoc's
cantrefs — stories of a place where all the seasons were mild, the
ground was fertile and the hunting far better than any known
before. And the new Gwynedd was a country where men could live
in peace free from the everlasting fears and effects of war, and from
incursions by the hated English.

When Madoc's people saw that the voyagers were intent upon
returning to this latter day Garden of Eden with their wives and
families, many others resolved to accompany them so that, in the
end, no less than ten ships assembled at Lundy Isle and sailed away.

And six hundred years passed before they were heard of again.

*   *   *

True or false? Before coming to a decision, one must consider the
'scientific' background. From time immemorial the belief existed
that the earth was flat and the sun moved round it. When the Christian Church evolved, it not only supported these contentions but
elevated them into doctrines. And since the philosophers of the so-
called 'civilized' world were either ecclesiastics or subject to the
strict control of Rome, these dogmas prevailed.

Even in 1492, the church warned Christopher Columbus that by
sailing westwards he would undoubtedly fall off the edge of the
earth and plummet to Hell. Still later, during the 16th century when

Galileo proved the Theory of Copernicus that the earth moved round the sun, the church condemned him for refuting its own belief that the converse was true. In order to reinforce its authority, the Holy Office threw him into jail but eventually had to bend with the wind of enlightenment which whistled round its ears. In order to save face, they released Galileo, making a 'deal' with him that he would recant his views and repeat the Seven Penitential Psalms every week for three years under pain of ex-communication. This enabled Galileo to return to the University of Padua where the new philosophy took root and eventually forced Rome to change its tune.

With medieval Wales being steeped in religion, Madoc would certainly have been brought up to accept these tenets without question. Thus, as a devout Christian, albeit that his beliefs may have been tinged with superstition, it is unthinkable that he would have embarked upon a voyage which would inevitably have resulted in his doom had he not been totally convinced otherwise. And since the only source of alternative logic in those days would have been of Druid or similar origin, the probability is that Madoc certainly met Mhaira and adopted her scientific philosophies.

A further proof of Madoc's voyage is to be found in a report concerning Morgan Jones, a cleric whose parish comprised the New York plantations. In 1686 he was captured by Indians of the Doeg tribe who roped him to a tree. As they made preparations for the ritual slaughter, Morgan began to pray in Welsh. Miraculously, his captors understood the language and promptly released him. It was then found that the nearby Padoucas tribe also spoke Welsh fluently and their ancestry was subsequently traced back to the *Madogwys*, i.e. the people of Madoc.

Another allusion to Madoc's migration came to light later in the 17th century when early settlers in North America came across the Madan tribe of Indians whose skins were much lighter than usual and who spoke in a tongue which strongly resembled medieval Welsh. Intensive research revealed reports substantiating Madoc's landing in Alabama during the 1170's at Mobile Bay where a memorial tablet has now been placed:

'IN MEMORY OF PRINCE MADOC, A WELSH EXPLORER, WHO LANDED ON THE SHORES OF MOBILE BAY IN 1170 AND LEFT BEHIND, WITH THE INDIANS, THE WELSH LANGUAGE.'

In view of the evidence, I feel that this Wondertale can only be regarded as being substantially correct.

Summit of Glyder Fawr

OWAIN GWYNEDD'S SILVER DAGGER

(A.D. 1170)

containing

The traditional but 'unlikely'
Legend of Idwal
together with its refutation

and

'The Aftermath' (Waterloo)
(A.D. 1798–1814)

THE 'UNLIKELY' LEGEND OF IDWAL

Owain Gwynedd was the most valiant and honourable of men.

In 1137, he succeeded his father as Prince of Gwynedd and during his long reign, welded the various, feuding factions within the Principality into a united nation. During this time he fathered 19 sons, one of the youngest being a handsome and intelligent boy named Idwal.

Since daughters were held in less esteem, with their births not always recorded, the exact number of Owain's offspring is unknown. One bard, though possibly to enhance his patron's virile reputation, revealed that his children numbered 36 in all.

For many years Gwynedd was engaged in a protracted war with Howel, the King of Powys, and Owain lived in constant fear that an enemy raiding party might penetrate his domain, capture Idwal, and hold him to ransom.

Accordingly, Owain turned to a distant relative named Nefydd, a harpist and bard of some repute who lived near Capel Curig, charging him to keep Idwal in the strictest, secret hiding and also instruct him in the arts of harp and song.

Now Nefydd was a handsome man and, like many successful bards, extremely vain, calling himself Nefydd Hardd, that is, Nefydd the Beautiful. He had a son called Dunawt who was plain of feature and slow-witted, yet his father's vanity was such that he judged the lad to be as beautiful as himself.

Following upon Idwal's arrival it didn't take long for Nefydd to realize that, in comparison, his own son appeared as ugly and stupid as the young prince was good-looking and clever, and this aroused such a bitter jealousy within him that he vowed to rid his household of one who revealed his own son in so poor a light.

One day Nefydd learned that Idwal was unable to swim and henceforth began to poison his son's mind with an intense hatred for his companion, gradually inculcating him with the idea of taking Idwal to the Nameless Lake above Llyn Ogwen and there, from the huge rock which projects from its western shore, push him into the water.

When Owain heard of his son's death he immediately instigated an Inquiry into the circumstances and though the evidence against Nefydd was serious, the Court was unable to prove his guilt. Irrespective of their decision, Owain considered that Nefydd had failed in his duty to ensure that no harm befell Idwal and sentenced him, together with all his descendents, to be reduced from the rank of gentlemen to bondsmen for evermore.

Thereafter, Owain became a bitter man and decreed that the lake should be named Llyn Idwal. And even the birds, sympathizing with the prince, refused to fly again over its deeply shadowed waters.

CHARGE AND COUNTERCHARGE

Although the story has been recounted thousands of times, neither the bards nor those who committed it to print in later years can have analysed the substance of the narrative which, examined logically, is self-destructive.

(1) From the historically accepted duration of Owain's marriage his wife could not have born 36 children. Hence, the inference that he was an adulterer and habitual lecher can be construed as correct, thus discounting one aspect of his 'honourable' reputation.

(2) Since Owain had nineteen sons of whom Idwal was one of the youngest, it is significant that special protection was afforded to him alone. This can only lead one to surmize that there must have been something remarkable about the boy's parentage and/or abilities.

(3) Historians have proved beyond doubt that Owain's two eldest sons, Hywell and Dafydd, were ruthlessly ambitious men whose lust for supreme power not only outweighed patriotism but transcended fraternal relationship. To this end, the brothers

gradually surrounded themselves with supporters, the two factions being mainly composed of those who were traditionally at odds with their rivals.

In his advancing years, Owain became increasingly disillusioned by the polarization of his subjects into two opposing camps. He realized that, upon his death, primogenital or elected succession would inevitably plunge the Principality into a civil war which the elders would be powerless to prevent thus permitting the King of Powys to conquer his domain piecemeal.

Accordingly, Owain took the unprecedented step of proclaiming Hywell and Dafydd as joint successors, a device designed to thwart their individual aims and so avert internecine strife. Furthermore, since neither could assume the title of Prince of North Wales, none of their descendants could claim automatic dynastic rights, leaving subsequent succession to the Elders.

This would leave the way open for the traditionally-minded Assembly to elect Idwal who would still be young enough to rule for a long period and ensure the stability of the realm.

Finally, to guard Idwal not only from the King of Powys but also from his eldest brothers who were openly contemptuous of their father's dark-haired favourite, Owain charged a trusted relative named Nefydd to ensure that no harm came unto him.

(4) The bards' assertion that Nefydd's educational duties be limited to instructing Idwal in harp and song must be considered in relationship to their own vocation wherein mastery of these accomplishments was regarded as the ultimate attainment. While Nefydd was certainly a bard of repute, he was equally a learned man, well versed in the politics of government and the arts of warfare. Thus the inference is that Nfydd was specifically chosen to groom Idwal for eventual leadership.

(5) The bards state that Owain instructed the Elders to hold an Inquiry into the manner of Idwal's demise. Since this was a personal rather than a state tragedy, it is unlikely that an autocratic ruler such as Owain Gwynedd would delegate jurisdiction to others. There can be little doubt that he would have judged Nefydd to be guilty of negligence in failing to ensure the boy's safety and put him to the sword, if not Dunawt as well, as a warning to others of the fate which lay in store for them and their families should they display dereliction of duty in discharging their leader's sacred trust.

Since Nefydd would realize this, it is beyond comprehension that he would seek to murder Idwal, or permit his life to be placed in jeopardy, during Owain's lifetime. On the other hand, neither Hywell nor Dafydd would have shed a single tear at their brother's

death leaving what, to them, was a relatively unimportant affair in
the hands of the Elders.

(6) It, therefore, stands to reason that Idwal's death took place after
Owain's and that Nefydd reported the fatality direct to the Elders, little doubt advancing a convincing story to absolve himself from
blame. This would necessarily be dependent upon the absence of
other witnesses whose evidence may conflict with his own. Accordingly, it is inconceivable that Dunawt was implicated in the felony
since, had he been present upon that fateful day, if he didn't 'crack'
under the stress of prolonged questioning, he would certainly have
done so when subjected to more sophisticated forms of interrogation. The chances are that Nefydd told the Elders that Idwal suddenly
ran into the notorious swamp at the southern end of the lake where he
was swallowed up in a matter of seconds.

(7) In their report, the bards assert that, 'through lack of evidence',
the Elders could not prove Nefydd's guilt. In the next breath,
however, they reveal Nefydd's intense jealousy (which, in itself,
could be construed as *prima facie* evidence as to motive), followed by
precise details of Nefydd's incitement to murder and Dunawt's
nefarious deed.

Since this evidence could not have been brought to light at the Inquiry, the question arises as to how the bards acquired these details.
Certainly neither Nefydd nor his son would have disclosed their involvement as this would have been tantamount to signing their own
death warrants. And with one or both being the sole witnesses of
Idwal's death — if crime there was — it must be concluded that the
bards' tale is pure fabrication from beginning to end.

(8) History confirms that following Owain's mysterious death,
Hywell and Dafydd immediately became rivals for power, civil war
ensuing, the government of the Principality being in the hands of
what can only be termed usurpers.

(9) Finally, there is one piece of evidence which totally destroys the
authenticity of this 'unlikely' legend. In A.D. 943, Howel Da issued
his Codified Laws wherein all men had their rank clearly defined
within a pyramid of five layers ranging from Chieftains down to
bondmen who lived on barren tracts of land which were inevitably
situated some distance from the principal centres of habitation.
It is a historical fact that the church of St Restitutius (St
Rhystyd in Welsh) at Llanrwst was built upon land given by one
of Nefydd's sons named Rhun. Even in those days, this could
only have been regarded as a 'prime' and valuable site. Thus
Rhun must have been a man of some substance and certainly not a
bondman or serf, a fact which repudiates the claim that Nefydd

and all his descendants were reduced in rank to the lowest of the low.

Hence it can only be concluded that the 'unlikely' Legend of Idwal is a cascading invention by a succession of over-enthusiastic bards who must have been sorely tried by the necessity of producing an endless stream of 'gripping yarns'.

In fairness, it should be remembered that they were the 'news reporters' of their times and would certainly seize upon 'front page stories' such as the mysterious death of their Prince, followed by the 'scandal' of his son's death, in no less an avid manner than some of today's newspapers. Unfortunately, in their desire to present 'exclusives', the bards let their imaginations run riot, substituting wild conjecture for facts.

The strangest aspect of this legend is that while it has a direct bearing upon Welsh medieval history, no one appears to have questioned its veracity, treating it almost as an adult fairy tale. It is, therefore, fortunate that the true and chronological elements of history have been preserved albeit embellished by a skilled mythologist who used the supernatural as a vehicle to enhance her own reputation.

In view of this I make no apology for including Mhaira's story in full, leaving the reader to sort out the wheat from the chaff. But a word of warning: everything is not quite as it appears. So don't jump to conclusions until you have read 'The Aftermath'.

OWAIN GWYNEDD'S SILVER DAGGER

At the head of Nant Ffrancon lies Llyn Ogwen from where an easy pathway rises to an amphitheatre of towering mountains beneath whose shadow lies a smaller lake which is now known as Llyn Idwal. This glacial legacy is a scene of savage grandeur unequalled anywhere in Britain. On mellow days it is a haven of strange beauty: but there are times when winds of terrifying power dart between the peaks driving dark clouds into the basin below where they writhe and swirl like spectral genies, whipping the water into angry waves twenty feet high before hurling the spume far into the valley beyond.

Long, long ago, this wild arena was the sole province of witches who dwelled in two deep caves set beneath a gigantic fracture in the rock formation which divides Y Garn from its neighbours, Glyder Fawr and Glyder Fach. And within this unclimbable schism blossoms a garden of high alpine flowers, the like of which is unknown elsewhere in the British Isles. Once this was the witches' hallowed garden. Then, as it is today, this brittle defect of nature was known as Twll Du, the original translation being The Black Cavern but now it is better known as the Devil's Kitchen.

The Coven of the Devil's Kitchen was unique, its members being highly educated women who were learned in Latin and Greek. Moreover, in addition to their devotion to Lucifer, they claimed spiritual affinities with the Teutonic gods such as Thor and Wodin, together with Roman, Greek and Oriental deities.

A short distance below the caves lay the nameless lake, unnamed since it was the ceremonial Place of Absolution wherein the Sisters washed away any taint of Godliness from their followers. And each afternoon, when the sinking sun silhouetted Castell y Gwynt — The Castle of the Winds — this Satanically sacred peak sent a long, triangular shadow across the entrances to the caves warning the Sisters that the time for the Observance of Ceremonies was at hand.

One day, the High Priestess, an ageless woman of great notoriety named Meghaira, was called to her eternal home by her guiding spirit, Mab, whereupon the others convened to elect a successor.

Now the Senior Sister of the Coven was a beautiful witch who, despite her thirty summers, looked far younger. And since she displayed unsurpassed skills in sorcery, performed miracles of materialization and spirit manifestations far superior to any other, and was also unequalled in the casting of horoscopes, spells and clairvoyant charts, Mhaira believed she would inherit the mantle of High Priestess. However, at dawn, when the oracle had spoken and smoke appeared through the Devil's Chimney, it was found that the remainder had unanimously elected the youngest witch, Bethan, a maiden of great beauty but possessing little occult powers.

The reason for this was not surprising. Twenty years previously Meghaira had appeared before Owain Gwynedd, the Prince of North Wales, in the guise of an exquisitely beautiful young woman. Together they climbed to the summit of the Glyders where she invoked Thor to create a tremendous storm from which they sought shelter amid Castell y Gwynt — where she seduced the Prince.

As a result of this interlude Meghaira gave birth to Bethan and the Coven had decided that the election of a Princess of the Realm as their High Priestess could only increase their influence and power in the land. But when Owain Gwynedd heard of this he was greatly troubled and retired to Beddkelert Priory to consider what should be done to curb the obvious ambitions of the Sisters.

As was only to be expected, Mhaira was exceedingly angry when she found that her claim had been passed over. Not only was she acknowledged to be the most accomplished witch but she genuinely felt that the Coven was meddling in political power at the expense of the spiritual and this would result in untold trouble. So, on the seventh day, she climbed to the Castle of the Winds and incanted the Supreme Ceremony of Invocation to her guiding Goddesses, Aphrodite, Venus and Diana, beseeching them seven times to intercede and atone for the misdeeds of her Sisters.

During the seventh visit, while making the Triple Supplication at precisely noon, Mhaira became aware that a mask was beginning to obliterate the sun. From her knowledge of astronomy she knew that a total eclipse of the sun was imminent and this she interpreted as a sign from the Prince of Darkness himself.

No sooner had the world grown black than she was seized by strong hands and forced to the ground. Since all the powers of the occult are nullilfied by a noon-time eclipse, save when this occurs on the Black Sabbath — that is, on the 30th April — Mhaira was unable to cast a spell upon her assailant and thus could not prevent him from having his way with her, all the time crying in his guttural voice: 'Vengeance is mine! Vengeance is mine!' But ere the skies lightened he fled so that she never saw his face.

Fearing that this was some degrading punishment meted out to her by Titan, she lay there trembling until the full light of day returned when the sun's rays struck a small, metal object lying nearby, the reflected glint of which caught her eye. Mhaira reached for the gleaming artefact and saw that it was a small, ornate, silver dagger, engraved with a strange design and having a peculiarly shaped hook protruding from the hilt. She had seen this pattern once before — on a talisman worn by Bethan and recognized it as the armorial symbol of the House of Gwynedd, worn only by the Prince and those of blood royal. And since she knew her attacker to be a man of mature years, it became obvious that she had been defiled by Owain Gwynedd himself.

At this, she prostrated herself upon the ground, petitioning her Goddesses that, in view of the terrible crime which had been perpetrated against her, they waive the rule that no spell could be cast against the father of a High Priestess. The Goddesses considered her request and pronounced their judgement.

First they decided that Owain had acted at the one time when she was unable to defend herself, thus revealing that at least one Protected Secret had been divulged unto him, thus making him a threat to the Sisterhood. Secondly, they held that he had ravished a

Sister, not out of lust but as an act intended to intimidate the Coven. And thirdly, since this attack was carried out in a place sacred to the Sisters, the crime was worthy of unprecedented punishment.

Accordingly, the Trinity of Goddesses decreed that Mhaira might punish this mere mortal in the manner she thought fit, granting their wronged Sister the power to cast one spell upon the Prince but made it a condition that she uttered this before leaving the sacred spot upon which she had been debased.

After offering a sacrifice for this precious gift of supreme power, Mhaira incanted her spell. . .

'Thou, Owain Gwynedd, prince of Gwynedd and father of Bethan, High Priestess of the Devil's Coven, adulterer and fornicator, desecrator of a Sister of Lucifer and the Sacred Temple of the Supreme Goddesses shall, before the moon waxeth full, be cast to the bottomless Pit of Acheron where, in those infernal regions, thou shalt suffer ever-lasting purgatory and the Hell-fire of Hades!'

Whereupon the wild winds blew, the sun became obliterated by clouds of purest black, jagged prongs of lightning streaked across the sky and, within a week, the prince was stricken by a fearful malady. Medics and priests were called to his side but neither potions nor prayers could alleviate his suffering. Now upon his father's death, Owain inherited a rare crystal which glinted brightly by day and night and, it was believed, not only possessed magical healing powers but turned dull when the Hand of Death was nigh. Owain sent for the crystal and clutched it in the palm of his huge hand. For a time all seemed well but on the seventh day the crystal turned dull and his last words were: 'The accursed Crystal of the Glyders!'

Some time previously, Owain had proclaimed his two eldest sons, Hywel and Dafydd, as his successors to rule jointly over the principality but, following his death, the brothers became rivals for power, and the prospect of civil war loomed ahead.

There were others, however, who knew that Owain's greatest wish was that his young son, Idwal, would eventually inherit the throne. In order to protect the boy from his elder brothers and also from the King of Powys, Owain handed him over to Nefydd, the truest and bravest of his kinsmen who had sworn to act as his foster-father and be responsible for teaching him the skills of harp and warfare and also imbue him with the requisite qualities of leadership.

Shortly after Owain's death, while Mhaira was making a sacrifice upon a new altar she had set up in Castell y Gwynt, she espied a young boy and a man ascending the path from Llyn Ogwen to the nameless lake. Although the distance was great, she perceived a device upon the boy's coat, recognizing it as the one engraved upon Owain's dagger.

She regarded the boy's companion intently. He was a man of proud stature, strikingly handsome and sporting a long, resplendent beard of purest gold. His powerful frame was extravagantly arrayed in a tunic and shirt of purple-brocaded silk sewn with golden thread, the fringes of his mantle likewise of golden silk, and a harp of gold was embroidered above his heart. Around his middle he wore a deerskin belt worked in gold thread, attached to which was a fine silver-hilted dagger in a sheath of figured cordwain. From his waist downwards were hose as green as the leaves of larch in spring, while his feet were encased in buskins of cordwain matching the sheath of his dagger and fastened with buckles of gleaming gold. Upon his head he wore a pointed hat, yellow as summer buttercups, with a tassel of emerald green. And his fingers were laden with rings of gold, many being set with precious stones.

'Little wonder that thou has added Hardd to thy name,' she soliloquized, 'for thy apparel alone advertizes a vanity too blatant for constancy.'

At this, she changed from her usual garb into the mode of attire worn by young peasant girls, rearranging her hair and proceeding to the outflow of the lake where it met the rising pathway. As the pair surmounted the rise she greeted them.

' 'Tis a beautiful day, Idwal-bach!' she said gaily.

'And a beautiful greeting from a beautiful girl,' the foster father replied, approving of what he saw. 'And what is thy name may I ask?'

'Thine eyes deceive thee, Nefydd Hardd,' Mhaira answered. 'I am but a poor peasant girl, though proud, you'll find . . . and they call me Glenda.'

'Thou art too modest,' came the gallant reply. 'Nor do mine eyes deceive me: they recognize beauty when they see it — beauty as wondrous as thy name.'

The banter had gone as far as Mhaira desired. 'Beauty thou mayest perceive,' she returned solemnly, 'but do not thine eyes deceive when they are blind to danger?'

'Danger? What danger be there here?'

'None here, my lord, but perhaps afar where those who covet power may be too ambitious.'

'Thou speakest in riddles, girl. Come! Of what ambition dost thou speak? Thine own, perhaps?'

Idwal, fascinated by water, had wandered to the lake edge so Mhaira moved close to Nefydd and spoke in a whisper: 'It is said that the rival brothers are gathering their lackeys about them.'

'What of it? Why should not a man surround himself with those he trusts?'

'No reason, sire,' she answered, 'but hast thou not noticed how they both exclude those who were closest to Owain Gwynedd?'

There was more than a grain of truth in what the girl said. This is no ordinary peasant, he thought.

'Idwal is but a child,' Mhaira continued. 'Will there be a throne for him when he comes of age?'

'A throne there will be.'

'But are there not those who seek to prevent him from sitting upon it?'

The idea had not occurred to Nefydd before.

'There are those whose ambitions are greater than their love for either Idwal or Gwynedd,' Mhaira intoned. 'In the highest places thou shalt see only a lust for power: in the lowly and humble, a love for this land greater than life itself.'

The man's arms encircled Mhaira's waist tightly. She spoke quietly: 'Owain Gwynedd died because he was a lustful man, an adulterer and fornicator who laid with Meghaira, the old High Priestess of the Devil's Coven, and fathered Bethan who is now the new High Priestess.'

'What!' A look of disbelief contorted Nefydd's face.

'Wouldst thou be as ignoble as Owain Gwynedd?'

'Owain was a noble man!'

Mhaira's lips distorted. 'Aye! Noble enough to have ravished me up yonder amid the Castle of the Winds!'

'Thou liest, girl!'

Mhaira took the Silver Dagger from her pocket. 'Dost recognize this?'

'Tis Owain's dagger!' he exclaimed. 'The one he lost shortly afore he died.'

'Lost it! It fell from its scabbard as he had his way with me!'

'Thy words bear the ring of truth, girl!'

'They are the truth! Doth this dagger lie?'

'Wilt thou swear?' he demanded.

'That I will! And upon the life of Olwyn of Dolwyddelan.'

'Thou knowest of her?' he asked incredulously.

'Yea! And of the future she foretold.'

'Since this you claim to know, repeat it so that I may judge whether or nay you are lying.'

'Was it not she who prophesied that if this dagger and its rightful owner should part company, he would die? And that the land of Gwynedd would fall into the hands of the usurpers?'

'Aye! That she foretold.'

'Then, my lord, wouldst thou seek to have thy way with me as Owain did . . . and with others, too?'

'Others?'

'Yea! Others!' Mhaira retorted. 'Many's the girl he waylaid in these mountains and whose firstborn was not sired by their husbands. And wives who have borne bastards in a shame unbeknown to their spouses! Nor dare they speak openly for fear of retribution!'

'Mother of Mercy!' The man crossed himself.

'And there's many a witch he took to his bed as well and many a child born unto them nine months later,' she confided.

She saw that her words were tearing away his credulity. 'Doth not this dagger prove that I tell the truth?' she demanded.

He agreed: it was undeniable evidence.

'Then there's another point, sire,' Mhaire continued. 'Was not Owain a tall man?'

'That he was and powerfully proportioned to match.'

'And fair?' she added. 'With eyes of blue and flowing silver hair which danced in the breeze?'

'That he had.'

'Was not Owain's wife fair also?'

He agreed once more.

'How old is the boy?'

'Twelve come December.'

'Is he not a small lad for his years?'

The man could only concur.

'And dark and swarthy with it, too?'

Nefydd was forced to admit that her observations were correct.

'Hast thou ever seen a woman in these parts who is not fair and possesseth a light complexion?'

'Only witches!' The response was uttered before he considered the implication.

'Aye! Only witches!' Mhaira returned triumphantly. 'And the boy is swarthy at that!'

'Art thou suggesting that Idwal be the bastard son of a witch?' he protested.

'Art thou suggesting that Bethan is not Owain's bastard daughter by a witch?'

Mhaira now had the man's reason at her mercy. 'Art thou

certain, my lord, that Idwal is the next rightful heir to Gwynedd?
Or was he returned to his father by the witch who bore him so that,
in time, the land of Gwynedd should be ruled by a Devil's Disciple
and half-brother to the High Priestess of the Devil's Coven?'

The man blanched as Mhaira slipped from his hold.

'Art thou merely a maiden, a sooth-sayer or a guardian angel in
disguise?' he stammered.

'I am only a peasant girl but with more sense than many a man,'
she replied. 'If what we both know to be the truth comes out, what
then?'

He confessed that there would be untold trouble in the land.

His mind, too, was now within Mhaira's grasp. 'Would it be
right for Gwynedd to be ruled by the son of a hag-witch? Or
wouldst not thou, the truest of Owain's kinsmen, be a more
honourable leader than either Idwal or the power-crazed coxcombs
who now vie for the throne?'

'How canst thou speak of me as an honourable man when I
would have been dishonourable enough to have taken thee?'

Mhaira took the man's hand and raised it to her lips. 'To desire
a woman is more natural than dishonourable,' she countered
warmly. 'But to ravish one is not! When I asked you to release me
you did so — and that was honourable. Thus thou art an
honourable man.'

'Thou art young to be a philosopher,' her escort said with a
smile, for her flattery had removed all doubt from his mind. 'What
would you suggest, philosopher?'

'Search your soul and mind. Then when you have seen clearly
that which must be done, strike the blow fearlessly, no matter how
bloody the act may be.'

'Wouldst that I had both thy mind and courage', he sighed.

'My mind thou shalt have,' Mhaira promised. 'But the courage
must be thine own — for without courage Gwynedd will fall into
the hands of the usurpers.'

At that, she drew back, calling out: 'I must away, sire, lest my
father fear that once more I have fallen into the hands of a man less
honourable than thee.' Turning, she tossed the Silver Dagger at his
feet, adding: 'Perhaps, this day, the dagger hath returned to its
rightful owner.'

Then she was gone up the long slope of Y Gribben.

From her vantage point high on the hills above the nameless lake,
Mhaira viewed the arena below. To the north-west, the steep slopes
of Y Garn merged with the lake, and beyond this dominant height
a rough track climbed between a myriad, tumbling boulders to the

mouth of the Devil's Kitchen. Straight ahead rose the Devil's pathway: to the left, the successive peaks of Glyder Fawr, Castell y Gwynt, Bristly Ridge and Glyder Fach stood proudly against the skyline while the rugged triangle of Tryfan completed the amphitheatre. Below this half-hidden, heather bestrewn mass, lay Y Gribben and, at the far extremity of this height, gigantic sloping slabs of stone, which seemed to descend from the clouds, reached the ground at a point where the pathway wended its way by the side of the lake. Opposite, half-way along the western shore, a huge rock protruded into the water with a smaller one, black and vertical, lying a little to the rear.

It was towards these rocks that Nefydd and Idwal meandered their leisurely way but from the manner of their progression it was obvious that the man was burdened with many problems.

'My mind thou shalt have!' The words leapt from Mhaira's innermost being. Summoning every vestige of power within her, she projected her thoughts towards him. Instantly, the man threw back his head as in pain and his hand passed across his brow. A sinister smile crossed her face.

'First I commanded thy admiration and then thy reason,' she mused to herself with a grimace. 'Next I made conquest of thy mind and ambition. Now I will control thy every act.'

When they came to the rocks, Nefydd sat by the smaller one, leaning against its smooth surface. He drew up his knees before him and covered his eyes with his hands, resting cool fingers on throbbing temples. Meanwhile, Idwal had wandered down to the lake and climbed upon the boulder projecting into the water, waving his hands, pulling faces and laughing at the weird reflections in the rippling surface below.

'Those who hold power may be too ambitious!' The message raced through Nefydd's mind.

'Hast thou noticed how they exclude all those who were closest to Owain Gwynedd?' The thought jarred his powers of concentration.

'Are there not those who would prevent Idwal from sitting upon the throne?' His mind became confused.

'In the highest places thou shalt see only a lust for power.' Another memory impinged itself upon his troubled train of thought.

'Owain Gwynedd was the father of Bethan, High Priestess of the Devil's Coven!' Beads of perspiration saturated his brow.

'Noble enough to ravish me, too!' The sarcastic, bitter words totally shattered Nefydd's erstwhile belief in Owain's honour.

'If the dagger and its rightful owner should ever part company the land of Gwynedd will fall into the hands of the usurpers!' Nefydd's hands slipped from his eyes. The Silver Dagger was now in his possession. If, perchance, he was the rightful owner and they should part company . . . he might die.

His senses reeled. His head shook from side to side.

'He's small for his years . . . and dark . . . and swarthy with it, too.' The man's judgement became a whirlpool and the vortex began to suck away all sensibility.

'Hast thou ever seen a woman in these parts who is not fair?' Fragments of clarity began to break away from a once lucid mind.

'Only witches!'

Nefydd's breathing became heavy: he clenched his teeth and his lips parted. He looked across at Idwal and watched the gyrations as the boy created distorted reflections in the lake.

'Art thou certain that Idwal is the rightful heir to Gwynedd?' Nefydd's breast rose and fell sharply, intelligence long departed.

'Or was he returned to his father by the witch who bore him so that, in time, the land of Gwynedd shall be ruled by a Devil's Disciple who is half-brother to the High Priestess of the Devil's Coven?' The beads of sweat upon his brow flowed, stinging, into his eyes.

'Would it be best for Gwynedd to be ruled by the son of a hag-witch?' The dagger twisted between damp fingers.

'Or wouldst not thou be a more honourable leader than either Owain's bastard son or the power-crazed coxcombs who vie for the throne today?'

Nefydd rose to his feet, leaned against the slab and raised his eyes to Heaven. Was not his allegiance due more to his country than the devil-boy now in his custody?

'Wouldst I had both thy mind and courage.' The memory became the cry of his soul.

'The courage must be thy own for without courage Gwynedd will fall into the hands of the usurpers.' The mind snapped, no longer capable of rational thought.

'The Silver Dagger hath returned to its rightful owner. . .! Its rightful owner. . . Its rightful owner. . .!'

The phrase drummed incessantly in his mind. The booming resonated within his head, stupefying, blinding. The sound magnified and the tempo increased until it coincided with the beat of his heart. A torturing pain pressed against his skull with an agonizing force. A torrent of ideas, rampaging incoherently through what was once sanity, became a maelstrom.

Were these not the words which Glenda, the peasant girl,

used? Or were they his own? Had there been a girl at all? Or was
he imagining the encounter? The past vanished from his life.
'From where did Nefydd Hardd obtain this dagger? Nefydd
Hardd! Who is he? Am I not that man? Or is he another? Had he
slain Owain Gwynedd? Or did I? Oh, no! I could not have done
it for I am an honourable man! But was not Nefydd Hardd also
honourable? And was not his allegiance to his country greater to
him than all else? For that matter, is it not mine also? Just like
Nefydd's', he reflected incoherently.
'What is that? Standing by the rock? 'Tis a boy . . . dark and
swarthy. A witch's bastard, no doubt! And what is he doing?
Casting spells upon the water, I'll be bound. And incanting silent
prayers to his half-sister in the Coven! Or unto the Devil himself!
Planning to destroy the Principality of Gwynedd and turn it into
the Devil's Dominion.'
By that time he was half-way between the slab and the rock,
moving unconsciously towards the boy.
'The Church would be destroyed, too. And all those who pray
therein forced to kneel before the Devil!' Nefydd's hand clasped the
dagger until his knuckles gleamed in the sunlight.
'Art thou like thy father, boy? With a penchant for witches?
Who would be the first, boy? Thy kinswoman, Bethan?'
Nefydd began to run, stumbling across the stones, his speed
increasing step by step.
'Aye! Thy half-sister it will be! Then thou canst thrust a half-
witted sorcerer incestuously upon the throne as thy successor? But
I'll do the thrusting first!'
Hearing the noise behind him, Idwal turned at the moment
Nefydd struck the blow, the dagger sinking into the boy's heart.
Yet the man's blundering progression had been so violent that, at
the moment of impact, he fell by the side of the rock. By the time
he regained his feet, Idwal had slipped into the water where his
body floated with the weapon still impaled in his heart. A moment
later the body sank and a lurid, crimson tint began to swirl around
the place of death, ever increasing in size.
The realization of what he had just done cleared Nefydd's senses.
'If the dagger and its rightful owner should ever part company
. . . the owner will die!'
An icy chill gripped his body. 'But am I the rightful owner?' his
mind questioned. 'Or was Idwal the rightful one?'
As from afar, a new reasoning entered his brain. 'Idwal and the
dagger have not parted company for the boy lies dead at the bottom of the lake with the weapon still in his heart. If he had been

the rightful owner then he would not have died for he has not been parted from the dagger.'

Fear now seized the man. Indeed, he argued, he — Nefydd Hardd — was the rightful owner and he and the dagger had parted company . . . for ever. Now he, too, would die. Had not Olwyn of Dolwyddelan so foretold? And did not her prophecies always come to pass?

Fear turned to panic as he raced towards the outflow of the lake. Yet, before he reached the path to Llyn Ogwen, the swirling, florid mass overtook him and ere he commenced his descent, the entire waters were blood red.

By the time Mhaira had traversed the pathway to the southern shore and reached the track leading to Twll Du, her Sisters were already there, wailing and calling upon Lucifer to interpret the meaning of this sanguine manifestation. At that moment Idwal's body floated to the surface, hovered there for a minute and then sank again.

'The Holy Grail!' cried one of the witches.

'It is a visitation from God,' another screamed.

'We are lost! We are lost!' Bethan lamented.

This was the moment for which Mhaira had waited. 'Silence!' she thundered. 'Call thyselves Sisters of Lucifer! Thou art no more than charlatans!' She turned to Bethan: 'And thee, High Sister, where is thy faith? Thou cringest like a wayward Christian being chided by a priest!'

Slowly, the Coven raised their eyes to the speaker.

'Harken unto me, thou weaklings!' Mhaira commanded. 'That was no Holy Grail! How could it be when that artefact is nothing but a part of Christian mythology? It was the body of a boy! Thrice it will rise and thrice it will sink, the last time for ever. When it shall next appear, let thine eyes look to its heart and seek the message contained therein.'

In silent fear the others watched until the body reappeared, seeming to hover upon a scarlet blanket before sinking once more.

'I saw a dagger!' cried one.

'I, too!' screeched another hag.

'It had Owain Gwynedd's crest upon it!' wailed a third.

'Aye!' Mhaira's voice rasped. 'Owain's dagger it was but now it hath become the dagger of death.'

The wailing started again with Bethan shaking from head to foot, scarcely having strength to stand.

'Oh ye of little faith!' Mhaira remonstrated. 'When the body rises again, regard its face.'

Suddenly the body broke through the shimmering red surface. A searing shriek echoed in the mountains as the High Priestess recognized Idwal and then collapsed to the ground, eyes and mouth wide open and her face a deathly white.

The wailing increased. Mhaira felt Bethan's temple. Though the beat was irregular, the girl was alive and that within a short space of time she would recover consciousness. But this precious hour, Mhaira realized, was a Hell-sent opportunity which she could never have anticipated.

She lashed her Sisters with the vilest epithet known to her sect. 'Children of God!' she stormed. 'Thou cringest like sinners before a Christian confessional while the High Priestess lies dead. So tarry here, all of you, like praying nuns! I, alone, will carry my Sister to the altar on Castell y Gwynt. When I return I shall bring her back with me, alive and well.'

'Bethan is dead!' cried one.

'Death is final!' wailed a yellowed hag.

'The dead cannot be resurrected!' wailed a third.

'What are life and death but changes in time and state,' Mhaira sneered. 'Poor, pathetic proselytes that you are! Before the sun sets you will have witnessed my limitless power — that of an *Arch-Priestess of the Prince of Darkness.*'

She picked up Bethan's inert body and carried it up the long traverse to Llyn Cwm — The Lake of the Dog — and then to the Castle of the Winds.

Bethan awoke to the sound of an Incantation which was new to her: a droning intercession which reverberated round the mountains.

'What art thou chanting?' she asked in awe.

'The Supreme Invocation for the Resurrection of the Dead,' Mhaira replied.

'Never have I heard an incantation of such power,' Bethan returned.

'Thou hast now, High Sister. Fortunately!'

'Is it for Idwal that thou chanteth?'

'I can do nothing for him. He is not one of us. That was for thee, Bethan-mawr.'

'Why for me?' the young witch asked tremulously.

'When you recognized Idwal, the mountains echoed with a shriek such as they have not heard since Olwyn's Dream. It was thine! Then you fell lifeless to the ground before the whole Coven. All our Sisters had such little faith that they could do nought but whimper like Christians at a funeral. So I carried thee here and beseeched our Master to give thee back thy life.'

'Why didst thou do that?'

'Why?'

To Bethan, Mhaira's voice sounded as though it was impossible for her saviour to have done otherwise. Guilt filled her mind.

'I believed that after being elected High Priestess you hated me,' she admitted.

Mhaira regarded her superior intently. 'What is the First Law of the Coven?' she asked.

'The Coven shall only worship the Prince of Darkness and carry out His works.'

'And what is the Second Law?'

'The High Priestess shall be elected by a majority of the Sisters therein.'

'Have I not acknowledged thee as such?' Mhaira queried.

Bethan agreed that she had.

'And the Third Law of the Coven?'

'That all the Sisters shall carry out the commands of the High Priestess, seek to preserve her and all other Sisters, neither harming each other nor any Sister of Lucifer.'

'Have I not done that, too?' Mhaira demanded.

Bethan could do no other but agree — for had not Mhaira resurrected her from the dead with a power which she knew was beyond her own. 'Where didst thou learn the Power of Resurrection?' Bethan entreated.

'Ah! That was many years ago', Mhaira began. 'Those who stood for the Christian idolatry seized three Sisters and bound them to crosses, placing great faggots round the bases, ready to burn them on the day of the Black Sabbath. As they lit the fires I brought down a deluge of rain such as those priests had never seen before. This put out the fires of death at the stakes and the fires of faith within their breasts so that they ran from the flood waters fearing their god to be wrathful. I was thus able to free my Sisters and lead them here to safety. As a reward, our Prince elevated me to the rank of Arch-Priestess with the power of resurrection over His Sisters.'

'That was a wond'rous thing to do, Mhaira-mawr,' Bethan said. 'Shouldst thou not then be the High Priestess of the Coven?'

Mhaira noted the addition of 'mawr' to her name: her superior now acknowledged her rank.

'Perhaps our Master would rather have me at thy left hand to guide thee so that, in the days ahead, while the High Priestess rules the spiritual world of Gwynedd, her kinsmen may rule the secular realm and perchance destroy the Christian church.'

'That can no longer be,' Bethan responded. 'Now that my brother is dead.'

'Thy brother!'

'Aye! Idwal was my natural brother, born unto my mother by Owain Gwynedd.'

Mhaira recovered from her surprise. 'Our Master works in ways we may not always understand,' she replied defensively.

'That is true', Bethan conceded. Then: 'What wouldst thou have me do next?'

'Return to the Coven and show our Sisters that thou art alive and well thus giving them renewed faith in our Master.'

Bethan agreed: it was the right thing to do.

As they descended the mountain, Mhaira spoke: 'I feel it would be wiser for thee to enter the abode alone rather than with me.'

'Why?' the girl asked. 'When thou hast given me life anew?'

'Not I,' the older woman advised. 'Only through me. Thy life was the gift of our Prince. Should we enter together, our Sisters, in their frailty, may attribute thy resurrection to me alone whereas thy rebirth was the will of Lucifer. That is the message they must hear from thy lips.'

For the second time Bethan agreed. Now she felt the need to have a Sister of such great wisdom at her left hand.

'There still remains the blood of Idwal,' Mhaira let fall.

'But what can we do? Was it not the will of our Master?'

'I doubt it,' the Arch-Priestess replied. 'I cannot think that He would pollute the waters of the nameless lake in such a manner.'

For the third time Bethan was forced to agree. Her admiration for her companion increased step by step.

'When thou hast spoken with our Sisters, I prithee descend to the rock where thy brother was slain and from there cast a spell upon the waters that they become clear again.'

Bethan found herself obeying for the fourth time. 'And I shall lead all the Sisters there so that they may behold such a great power of magic that it will restore their faith.'

'Beware, Bethan-mawr,' Mhaira warned. 'Would it not be wiser if we went there alone perchance the time is not ripe for a miracle. If the day is not auspicious and thou shouldst fail, may not our Sisters, in their present state of doubt, fear that death has taken away thy powers?'

It was now the fifth time that the High Priestess saw the infinite prudence of the older woman's mind. 'Aye, Mhaira-mawr,' she conceded, 'thy words are the wisest.'

By then they had reached the junction of the traverse where Bethan left her Sister and ascended to the caves while the other proceeded to the lake. An hour elapsed before she joined Mhaira at the Rock of Death.

'If thou art ready, little mother,' her mentor urged. 'Chant quietly lest others hear and later ask what you were doing.'

Six times Bethan had now agreed. Was there no end to this woman's wisdom? Quietly she began a whispered chant of magic to restore the waters to their former state: chanted and chanted until darkness fell and the moon waxed bright: invoked, incanted and made supplication; ordered, demanded and pleaded until she could no longer speak.

At last Mhaira turned to Bethan: 'Tis midnight and the waters still run red. Perhaps thy powers were weakened by thy death and resurrection.'

The High Priestess could only agree. Worse still, she felt that the power of magic no longer remained with her.

'Worry not,' Mhaira said kindly. 'A miracle as great as this requires magic of the highest degree: perhaps a sacrifice.'

For the seventh time Bethan agreed and thanked her Prince for having sent Mhaira to sit at her left hand.

'Pray grant me permission to leave the Coven until the next full moon,' Mhaira requested. 'Then, the following dawn, the blood of thy brother will have disappeared from the lake and the waters will run clear again.'

'But how canst thou achieve this?' Bethan asked, somewhat taken aback. 'Would not the Master have given me the power if this was His will?'

'Ah, you forget, Bethan-mawr, that I am an Arch-Priestess sent to serve thee until thy own powers reach maturity.'

Of course this was true. Her wise adviser must be allowed to go at once.

And, as the High Priestess ascended to her cave, the Arch-Priestess set out to achieve the greatest magic of all.

On leaving the lake, Mhaira made her way down to the valley and climbed to a secret cave set high in the cliffs of Gallt yr Ogof where she spent the night. The following morning she again assumed the appearance of Glenda and journeyed to Beddkelert. Night was falling when she arrived at the Priory and sought shelter until the morrow. On admittance, she enquired if Nefydd Hardd was present.

'Whoever is Nefydd Hardd?' the monk enquired.

'A kinsman of our blessed Owain Gwynedd and in mortal peril,' she confided.

'What makes thee think he would come hither?'

'He is a pious man, brave and honourable, appointed foster-father to Idwal ap Owain Gwynedd. Knowing that his life is in danger I felt that he would seek sanctuary here or upon Bardsey Isle.'

'Ah, yes! I know of that man but he dwells not here,' the venerable monk replied. 'Tell me, my girl, whatever couldst thou do to assist him?'

'I carry a message which will remove the danger hanging over him.' Then, seeing the old man's eyes show interest: 'If he tarries not here I must away to Bardsey Isle before it is too late.'

She turned to go but he restrained her. 'My child! Thou canst not travel abroad at this late hour lest others waylay thee for their own purpose. Tarry here and depart at dawn.'

'Time waits for no man,' she answered. 'Neither does death. This is a matter which cannot go unattended for a moment.'

Her display of impetuosity and sincerity removed the monk's remaining doubts. 'Come with me,' he commanded. 'I will take thee to the Prior's cell.'

As Mhaira entered she heard the old man reading from a prayer book in Latin. He became silent when she joined in the ritual prayer which she knew by heart.

'Thou art a scholar, then?' he asked.

'I speak Latin and Greek,' came the startling reply, 'but I need to speak in my own language with Nefydd Hardd.'

'I have sworn that I will not disclose his whereabouts . . . but if you will send a message. . .'

'And the answer?'

'Thou shalt have it by dawn.'

Mhaira knew that a verbal message must be sufficiently baited to lure Nefydd to her retreat. Equally, it must be couched in terms which left both Prior and messenger ignorant of its full meaning.

'I prithee, mark every single word well,' she requested.

The Prior commenced to write as Mhaira dictated: 'What lay in the heart of Bethan's brother beneath Llyn y Dyfroedd will be restored to its rightful owner within Gallt-yr-Ogof Uchaf on the night before the next full moon.'

'I make no sense of that,' the Prior declared. 'I have never heard of a bloody-watered lake nor an upper cave at Gallt-yr-Ogof.'

'If this man be Nefydd Hardd he will understand it.'

'God be with thee,' the ancient blessed.

'And with thy messenger also!' Though, to a witch, the thought of putting any trust in the Prior's master was almost too much to bear.

Next day, Mhaira received an assurance that Nefydd would meet her at the appointed place and time whereupon she departed to her cave.

Once within her mountain sanctuary Mhaira started to knit a narrow tube from the finest wool, using needles no thicker than the stem of a daisy. She worked throughout the entire day until, by nightfall, this tube — no wider than half-an-inch — was over fifteen feet long. Next day she fastened hollow rush reeds end to end, pushing the wider ends over the narrower ones to produce a tube equal in length to the woollen one. She then sealed the joints of the rush tube with a resin-like concoction made from pig's trotters, milk and boiled fish, slipping the larger tube over the reed one, and waterproofing the whole with pitch. To one end of the tube she attached a lump of dried bark impregnated with tallow; for the other end she fashioned a circle of cowhide with a hole in the centre through which she passed the double tube and bonded the whole together, again with pitch. Next she wove a strong net in the manner of a pouch with ends long enough to tie round a man's middle.

Later, she emerged from the cave and procured two lengths of rope which she stored with her apparatus before obtaining a dry log, large enough to support a man in water, and placing it by the rock overhanging the nameless lake. When all her preparations were complete, Mhaira awaited Nefydd's arrival.

He entered the cave and caught his breath at the sight of the young peasant girl cooking a meal over an open fire.

'What art thou doing here?' he demanded.

'Preparing to return the Silver Dagger to its rightful owner.'

'Is it here, then?'

'Have patience', Mhaira replied. 'There is yet a little work to be done before the power lies in your hands.'

'Where is the dagger now?'

'Tis where you left it, sire.'

'How knowest thou where I left it?' he exploded.

'I saw a man of great courage put the land of his birth before all else. Gwynedd will have a fine Prince upon its throne . . . when you sit upon it.'

'And the dagger?'

'I know exactly where Idwal's body lies.'

'If the dagger is still at the bottom of the lake, how can it be returned to me?'

'Eat of my poor fare, sire, and whilst you fill your belly I will inform you.'

'If this is a trick, girl, I'll drown thee in the lake as I did the boy.'

She ignored his rough threat. 'I once served Olwyn of Dolwyddelan and she taught me many things. Including how to walk beneath the sea,' she let fall.

'That is not possible.'

As Nefydd ate his supper, Mhaira unfolded her plan. She showed him her handiwork.

'This is a breathing tube,' she explained. 'One end of it is placed in the mouth while the other end floats on the surface of the water being supported by the bark. I have measured the depth of the lake and this device is more than ample.'

Nefydd stopped eating. 'Did Olwyn tell you of this?'

'That she did! It is an ancient Egyptian invention with which a man may stay submerged for a whole day provided he first blocks his nose with tallow. They often used it when acting as spies.'

'Ah, Glenda! Thou art surely as clever as though art beautiful. Pray tell me, how do I reach the bottom of the lake and rise to the surface afterwards.'

'By the lakeside I have placed a dry log, large enough to support your weight in water while you paddle four paces from the rock with one end of the rope fastened round your waist and the other passed over the log and secured to a convenient tree nigh unto the rock itself. This net is to wear round your middle with a heavy stone placed within it. When I pay out the rope, the weight of the stone will take thee to the bottom. As soon as you have recovered the dagger, tip the stone from the net, tug once on the rope, push on the bottom with thy feet and I will haul on the rope and thus assist in drawing thee up to the log and thence to the shore. With this second rope I will secure myself to another tree perchance I fall into the water by accident.'

A broad grin spread over Nefydd's face. 'I'll warrant Olwyn did not tell you that!'

'Did not I warn you that I had more sense than many a man?'

'And so thou hast, my girl. Yet I, too, can make plans. Wouldst thou have me as the wisest Prince ever to rule over Gwynedd?'

'That I would, sire.'

'To be a man of that stature I would need the dagger in my belt, thy wisdom sitting on my throne by day and thy beauty lying in my bed at night. What sayest thou to that, Glenda?'

'Art thou asking me to be thy wife or thy woman?'

'My wife! Then no other may share thee.'

'Thou makest the prettiest of speeches, Nefydd Hardd. And when wouldst thou wed me?'

'I'll wed thee tonight, my love, and tomorrow see the priest.' He seized her roughly.

'Nay, my love,' she responded. 'Tomorrow night there is much work to be done. I'll none have thee so weary that you drown in the lake.'

'Oh, Glenda! There is the morrow for resting.'

'Be not like Owain Gwynedd, Nefydd. First the dagger, then seek out the priest, whereupon you will discover that I shall love thee in a fashion more wonderful than thou hast dreamed possible.'

'Thou art right, girl. First the dagger, next the priest and finally the throne.'

On the morrow, when darkness fell, they carried their equipment to the nameless lake and thence to the rock. Nefydd divested himself of his jacket, shirt and boots, tied one end of the rope round his waist and the other to a jagged rock, passed the rope over the log and prepared to enter the water.

'Give me thy heavy belt and dagger,' Mhaira whispered. 'There's one too many daggers in the lake already.'

He handed them to his companion and slipped into the water. 'How shall I see below the surface?' he enquired suddenly.

'The moon hath now waxed full, my prince. Its light, reflected by Pen yr Ole Wen,[1] will penetrate to the bottom. What is red during the day is but soft pink by moonlight.'

He paddled to the place which Mhaira indicated and dropped out of sight, only the floating bark showing his position. The minutes passed slowly. At last, she felt a tug on the rope at which she hauled until Nefydd's head appeared, followed by his hand holding the dagger.

'The Silver Dagger hath returned to its rightful owner!' he shouted triumphantly as she dragged him towards the shore. 'I'll give thee thy reward tonight, my fine girl!' he cried as he reached the rock. 'We'll wait for no priest now!'

Mhaira shuddered at the threat to which she was not prepared to submit. As Nefydd hauled himself up the slippery surface she reached for his own dagger and thrust it into his heart. Instantly, the Silver Dagger fell from the man's hand and sunk to whence it came and, as Nefydd's blood mingled with the ruddy waters, the lake began to lighten in colour.

Mhaira then proceeded to complete her task. She replaced the murderous weapon in its sheath, dressed her victim's body and fastened the belt round his middle. Next she filled the net with stones, tied the rope to the log, draped Nefydd across it and propelled it away from the bank. A moment later she pulled

Lyn Idwal and Pen yr Ole Wen

sharply on the rope causing the log to cast its burden to the bottom
of the lake. Finally she tied the ropes and breathing tube to a rock
and hurled them into the lake, casting the log in the undergrowth.

'Revenge is now mine, Owain Gwynedd!' she soliloquized. 'No
longer can thy knowledge of the Protected Secrets shackle the
Coven with chains of fear. Nor can Idwal learn them from his
sister. The Silver Dagger — the power behind the throne of
Gwynedd — is gone forever and Nefydd Hardd can never implicate
me. Only my Master and I know where the dagger lies and there
it shall remain unless He, in His infinite wisdom, performs a
miracle without precedence and restores it to the one of His choice.'

Then she swept up the pathway to Castell y Gwynt. There she
saw that the lake had already returned to its former crystal
clearness. She addressed her Master:

'Prince of Darkness, who reigneth in Hell, glorious be Thy name;
Thy Kingdom come and Thy Will be done in Gwynedd as it is in
Hades: give unto me this day the power to serve Thee, forgiving
the weakness of Thy Sisters so that I may show them the way to
Thy Kingdom, Thy Power and Thy Glory, world without end,
Amen.'

And though the Arch-Priestess in her spiritual euphoria did not
hear the reply, Lucifer was already making plans for her to do just
that.

At dawn, Bethan and her Sisters perceived Mhaira striding down
from the Castell, while before them lay the clear waters of the Lake
of Absolution. The High Priestess greeted her mentor: 'Come
Mhaira-mawr, walk with me while you describe this miracle,
teaching me likewise of thy magic so that I may serve the Master
in a better fashion.'

'It required a sacrifice.'

'What manner of a sacrifice, Mhaira-mawr?'

'A human one.'

'A human sacrifice! But who?'

'Dost thou remember the words of Olwyn of Dolwyddelan who
said that he who holds the dagger holds the power. And if the dagger and its rightful owner are parted, the owner would die?'

'That I have heard.'

'It crossed my mind that some ambitious man either stole the
Silver Dagger from Owain — which because of Olwyn's prophecy
was hardly likely — or administered some potion unto him in order
to gain possession of the artefact.'

'But Idwal would never do that!'

'That is so but neither would he kill himself. So whoever held the dagger after thy father's death, killed thy brother. Thus I became suspicious of Idwal's foster-father who had a Christian hatred of witches and those he called the bastard sons of witches.'

'Then he was aware of Idwal's parentage?'

That was a difficult question. Mhaira realized that if others learned how she came by the dagger and then subsequently gave it to Nefydd, she could be accused of complicity in Idwal's death.

'That was something I knew not so, following upon thy father's death, I transformed myself into a beautiful young girl and met Nefydd by yonder path. By use of women's wiles I discovered that he was wearing the empty scabbard of Owain's dagger in his belt,' Mhaira announced triumphantly.

'Then he killed my brother?'

'That he did! But he was careless enough to leave the weapon in Idwal's body and, knowing of Olwyn's foretelling, fled in fear of his life. Not that this was necessary for he was never the rightful owner.'

'What has this to do with thy great miracle?'

'I believed that Nefydd should atone for his crime. Now when a man waits for death he will clutch at a straw. I tracked him to Beddkelert Priory from whence I lured him here with the promise of my favours and the return of the dagger. Now he hath suffered the same fate as befell Idwal, his blood propitiating the sin and clearing the waters.'

'Thou truly art a great witch,' Bathan responded.

'I am here but to serve thee and our Master,' Mhaira replied.

'Now that Nefydd's body lies at the bottom of the lake, is it right for its waters to be used in the Ceremony of Absolution?' Bethan enquired.

'I would think not.'

'Then how can we cease to hold the Ceremony here without others asking the reason? If the Elders discover that Idwal's foster-father lies there — thou knowest what that may mean!'

'Since thy brother lies there also, would it not be propitious to name the lake Llyn Idwal in his memory, a matter which would be looked upon with favour by all. For Absolutions we could use the Little Llyn Cwn instead.'

'Oh, thou art wise beyond my wisdom.'

'As to the slabs, I suggest that henceforth they be known as the Idwal Slabs and thus remain forever as the memorial stones of thy brother's grave.'

Bethan agreed: her gratitude was boundless.

The next day, a ceremony was held to give the lake and the slabs

The Idwal Slabs

their eternal names. At the end of the service Bethan called upon the birds of the Principality to obey her Ordinance that, as a mark of respect for her dead brother, they should never again fly over Llyn Idwal.

And it came to pass that the birds obeyed her wishes and Bethan took Mhaira to live with her that she might receive constant instruction in the realm of magic.

A few days later, Mhaira informed Bethan that Lucifer had spoken to her pronouncing it to be His Will that Bethan's son should rule over the Principality while she held sway in the spiritual sphere. In that way the Christian church with all its idolatrous rites could be destroyed forever and those who lived in the land would find the Truth Eternal.

Bethan agreed without hesitation but expressed uncertainty as to how this could be achieved.

'I am to seek a man of Owain Gwynedd's stature who hath blue eyes and flowing silver hair. When I return with him you must lure him to the summit of Glyder Fawr where thou shalt call upon Titan to bring about a mighty thunderstorm from which ye shall shelter in the Castle of the Winds. There you shall seduce him and conceive his child. And with you being tall and fair like your father, you shall bring forth a child who is also tall and fair rather than swarthy, dark and small of stature as was Idwal. When your condition is confirmed it can be announced that you are carrying Owain Gwynedd's child which, by the Grace of God, he placed in thy womb before he departed this life.'

'Dost thou think they will believe a witch?'

'Nay, Bethan, that they will not,' Mhaira replied. 'Hence thou shalt live in the cottage where Olwyn of Dolwyddelan once abode, still transformed as a peasant girl. Then, when the period of suckling is over, the child can be handed directly to the Elders of the Realm. And with him being in Owain's image, they will guard him faithfully until he is old enough to ascend the throne. Thereafter, the future is in our Master's hands.'

'But how can we ensure the father's silence?'

'If, in order to ensure that Gwynedd enters the realms of our Master, the martyrdom of one Christian is a small price to pay for their deliverance from idolatry,' Mhaira declared.

'But what of the man's body?'

Mhaira indicated the lake. 'Henceforth the Waters of Absolution shall be the Waters of Sacrifice.'

Bethan agreed. 'Thy words are wise, great sorceress. When dost thou propose to leave?'

'There is no time to be lost otherwise we may have people questioning the length of thy pregnancy.'

And with that Mhaira departed upon a journey which took her over the length and breadth of Gwynedd but never did she see a man who equalled Owain in stature and possessed eyes of blue and silken hair which danced in the breeze. Eventually she reached the uttermost limit of the Principality and followed the River Dee in the direction of Chester which was garrisoned by soldiers who were native to the Pennines of England and, being of Scandinavian descent, were tall and fair.

As she traversed the sands she came upon a seagull which had been attacked by a bird of prey and, though mortally injured, was struggling to reach a crevice in the high bank. As the bird approached this sheltered enclave it collapsed and died but even in death it had led Mhaira to its nest wherein three fledglings lay with beaks open and ravenous. Feeling that, in death, the seagull had led her to life, she interpreted this as a sign for her to stay and feed them until they were old enough to fly. The young birds, owing their lives to the witch, came to regard her as their mother, staying with her constantly wherever she went.

Meanwhile, the Arch-Priestess visited Chester where she found a corporal who fulfilled all her requirements. Bewitching him with promises of pleasure and wealth beyond his wildest dreams, he followed Mhaira to Llyn Idwal.

There, Bethan carried out Mhaira's instructions following which she took the man to live with her in the cottage to ensure that conception took place. But such was his way with her that she had no desire to see him depart.

When it was confirmed that she was with child she informed Mhaira of her intention to live with him until such time as the suckling was completed.

The Arch-Priestess was most displeased with this arrangement since she knew how people talked and it would be impossible to support the story that the child had been sired by Owain Gwynedd. It was also obvious that Bethan was besotted by her lover and, in living with him, she was not only disregarding her duties within the Coven but was also renouncing her vows.

Next day, while the soldier was fishing, he was approached by an old woman who said she was too poor to buy food and begged just one small fish for her supper, offering him, in return, a potion which she claimed would increase his virility to such an extent that women would become his slaves forever. The soldier, being more than pleased with the bargain, gave her two fishes, drunk the potion and within the hour was dead.

That evening Bethan returned to the Coven afflicted by grief and anger. As she passed Llyn Idwal she noticed three seagulls flying above its waters and immediately summoned the King of the Birds and asked him why his subjects were disregarding her ordinance. The bird, a wise old seagull from Llanfairfechan, assured Bethan that these were not birds which dwelled in Gwynedd but hailed from Britain from whence they had come with the new High Priestess of the Coven, a woman named Mhaira.

At this, Bethan entered the smaller of the two caves where, as she expected, she found the Arch-Priestess. 'So! Thou hast set thyself up as High Priestess!' she challenged the older woman.

Mhaira nodded in response.

'On what authority?' Bethan thundered.

'The Sisters saw thou hadst renounced thy vows by living with a man and also perceived that no longer did thy ordinances have any power.'

'To what ordinances dost thou refer?' Bethan demanded.

'Even the birds no longer acknowledge thee,' Mhaira answered disdainfully. 'See how they fly over thy brother's grave.'

'Have the Sisters elected thee?'

'It was not necessary.'

With that, Bethan stormed out of the cave and entered the larger one where the remainder of the Coven were seated, there recounting what the King of the Birds had told her and railing at her Sisters for allowing themselves to be deceived by trickery. Then, as the High Priestess they had elected and who could never be dismissed from office, she called upon them to punish Mhaira for having usurped her authority by deception. Threatening them, too, that if they did not obey her commands, she would bring down the wrath of Lucifer upon their heads.

With this supreme threat hanging over them they rose as one and seized Mhaira, dragging her down to the lake and the Rock of Death. There they flung her into the depths of the Sacrificial waters, at once averting their eyes and returning to their cave to make penance before their leader.

As soon as Mhaira broke the surface, three young seagulls swooped down and took her hair in their beaks, holding her head above water so that she did not drown. Then they settled upon the lake beside her and swam towards the eastern shore, pulling her along until she was able to clamber from the lake on to the pathway. As she stood erect, she felt a pricking sensation in the small of her back and, passing her hand behind her, found that a sharp metal object had attached itself to the cord about her waist. Sliding it round to the front, Mhaira discovered that when she hit the bottom of the lake, the hook of Owain Gwynedd's Silver Dagger had caught itself on the cord and, as she fingered it disbelievingly, she heard a voice from Castell y Gwynt: 'The Silver Dagger hath now returned to its rightful owner.'

When Mhaira recovered from her ordeal she ascended the Castle of the Winds, this time taking the steep, trackless route over Y Gribben, so that she could not be seen from the Devil's Kitchen. Once there, she paid homage to her Master for having made intercession on her behalf and so enabling her to continue His works, celebrating the Thanksgiving of Supernal Resurrection, the Apotheosis of Hell, and the Penance of Atonement.

Thereafter she addressed her Prince, charging Bethan with two most serious transgressions. First, that whereas the Fifth Ordinance of Sisterhood incorporated the Vows of Chastity, save for the sole purpose of conceiving daughters to ensure the continuance of the Sisterhood, or sons to be raised as Devil's Disciples, the High Priestess had indulged in Concubinage by living with a man in a licentious relationship to the complete exclusion of her religious duties. Secondly, that Bethan had broken the Third Law of the Coven in that she failed to preserve the life of a Sister and sought to bring harm unto her.

The Prince of Darkness listened unto his devotee and then replied: 'All this is known to me. That the High Priestess has violated her vows of celibacy is a depravity which invites severe punishment: that she neglected her duties is a sin of even greater degree: but in seeking to end the life of a Sister is the inexpiable crime which must attract the ultimate penalty. And this punishment shall be suffered not only by her but also by all those who aided her in this nefarious act.'

No sooner had the Prince spoken than the mountains echoed and re-echoed a tremendous, sickening crack as the rock face above the Devil's Kitchen opened up in a quivering schism, the pillars of which hovered for a moment before plummeting down upon the caves, disintegrating as they fell in a violent, traumatic torrent of tumbling boulders. When the dust finally settled and silence prevailed, the caves and the Coven had disappeared forever.

Lucifer spoke again: 'As to thee, Arch-Priestess, now I can explain matters concerning which you know not fully. Meghaira, the last High priestess, was little better than her daughter, Bethan. When she seduced Owain Gwynedd she found him so greatly to her liking that she also broke her vows of celibacy and formed a permanent relationship with him. This I tolerated since, at first, she was meticulous in the observation of every other duty and I hoped that she might be able to influence this man in such a way that he would destroy the priesthood in his domain. But this she never attempted to do, such was her infatuation. Instead, in her efforts to retain his favours, she betrayed unto him some of the Protected Secrets of the Sisterhood, thus making him a threat to their existence, this eventually resulting in the entire Coven at Conwy being destroyed.

'In retaliation, I sent Bethan unto his enemies disguised in the mantle of a nun and she informed them that Owain's personal priests, who dwelled in a certain monastery, were — in reality — his soldiers in disguise. As a result, the English massacred the priests. Foolishly, Bethan then boasted that they had avenged their Sisters' deaths.

'Accordingly, Owain Gwynedd, with the knowledge gained from the Protected Secrets, demanded that Meghaira disclose unto him the identity of the Sister who was responsible for the slaughter. In order to please this man and also to shield her daughter, she said that you were my emissary. In punishment for this sin, Mab recalled Meghaira and consigned her to purgatory for ever.

'When Bethan became the new High Priestess, Owain Gwynedd devised a most sinister plot designed to subjugate her to his will. Knowing that a Sister cannot defend herself during the sun's eclipse save on the Black Sabbath, he decided to rape thee at that hour, thus avenging the deaths of his priests. That is why he cried: 'Vengeance is mine!'.

'But there was a far more devious reason for perpetrating this act. He knew that when Bethan heard of your defilement she would henceforth believe that his powers were greater than those of any Sister and, thereafter, be afraid to oppose him, becoming subject to his every whim and command.

'Fearing that this man may seek to harm thee further I instructed Vesta to watch over you and, seeing thy plight, she informed me instantly. Thereupon I seized the opportunity which presented itself and, at the moment when he was quite incapable of giving thought to material things, I caused the Silver Dagger to fall from his scabbard. Then, with the power in thy hands, I left all matters to thee in the knowledge that thou, the most faithful of my servants, would destroy the House of Gwynedd for ever.

'For thy assistance I sent Aphrodite, Venus and Vesta in the form of three seagulls to protect thee. And it was fortunate that I did, for in serving me so faithfully, thou hast suffered greatly. Thus I shall reward thee with as great a trust as I have ever subordinated to anyone. . .

'Thou shalt journey to a place nigh unto the Druid's Circle on Rombald's Moor in the West Th'Riding of Yorkshire. Nine leagues south from this hallowed ground there is a deserted cottage in which thou shalt take up thy abode and which shall be named the Devil's Elbow. While there I charge thee to gather all the lore and legends, the histories of the hobgoblins, and all the witches' tales pertaining to the West Th'Riding and so become the first Keeper of Lore and Legend.

'Nor is that all. Thy second duty is of the greatest import. The power contained in the Silver Dagger is not confined to Gwynedd but encompasses the entire universe. I charge thee to keep it safely through what may be an eternity of time until one day thou shalt meet a giant of a man with eyes of blue and silver hair which dances in the breeze. When he stands before thee, thy everlasting spirit will immediately recognize him as the next rightful owner.

'Unto him shalt thou give the Silver Dagger and with it the power to change the course of history as thou has done. And unto him must thou impart all the lore and legend of which thou art the keeper.

'But verily I warn thee. There is one place in that Th'Riding where neither Saint nor Satan dares to tread and upon which thou must never set foot lest thy soul be lost forever. Mark well its name, Soyland Moor, for the first son to be born amid this savage scene of desolation will be that man.'

Straightway Mhaira journeyed unto the cottage where her Spirit and Traits lived on for a span of years unknown since Methuselah. . .

Until one day, seven hundred years later, when the wild wind howled across the moorland and the ensuing blizzard forced man and beast alike to seek shelter. Then, as the leaden skies darkened into night, there was a knock upon her door and, opening it, she saw a man standing before her . . . tall and fair, with eyes of blue and flowing silver hair. . .

At last she had met that man.

*   *   *

Despite Mhaira's immediate acceptance of her visitor she was surprised by his youth and by his patronymic, Tom o'Soyland, which was more often used than his real name of Tom Brackenridge.

THE AFTERMATH

From 1801 to 1808, Tom Brackenridge lived near Grasmere, Cumbria, where he established a love — hate relationship with William Wordsworth and his sister, Dorothy. Despite their esteem for his abilities, they never referred to Tom in their writings, though a study of their lives leaves little doubt as to their motives in concealing this acquaintanceship.

First, William was inordinately fascinated by tales of presentiment and the occult, these either terrifying him or resulting in his sexuality being stimulated to an abnormal degree. Any reference to licentiousness and, in particular, to virgins being ravished in their open graves prior to being sacrificed, roused his carnality in a monstrous and ghoulish fashion.

This is born out by two references in Dorothy's Journals dated the 29th and 30th April, 1802, the latter being the infamous Black Sabbath. She vividly describes how, on the 29th, at William's insistence, they both lay in a trench under a fence: 'he thinking it would be sweet thus to lie as in a grave. . .' After this episode, Dorothy wrote that she was sick and ill and (which was unusual) slept alone.

Next day they returned to the hollins where, immediately upon their arrival, William spread a cloak upon the ground. Dorothy describes how she regarded the prospect as in a vision. 'I was so resigned to it!' she wrote. Obviously the traditional Black Sabbath sacrifice had not only been planned but grotesquely rehearsed the previous day.

On the 22nd August 1801, Tom dined with the Wordsworths to whom he recounted the story of Owain Gwynedd's Silver Dagger in its entirety. As the story progressed, William's breathing waxed short and heavy. When the saga ended, for full dramatic effect, Tom slapped the dagger on the table whereupon the poet turned white and shook violently.

Tom challenged him, as the greatest living poet, to transform the prose into an epic poem but William declined fearing that 'this would bring down the wrath of God upon his head'. Feigning indigestion, he forthwith retired to bed.

Seeing her brother's distress, Dorothy pleaded with Tom never to reveal William's weaknesses and superstition. In return, she volunteered to instruct him in the art of keeping Journals in such a manner that while they were totally comprehensible to the writer, the exact truth would be denied to others who may subsequently have access to them. Furthermore, she swore that she would never include in her diaries anything which referred to him.

The second motive for the Wordsworths' silence is more insidious. After studying Dorothy's Journals in depth, Tom finally broke down the pattern of sophistry she employed in her writings wherein she used euphemisms and innuendo to blanket the naked truth . . . not only that she had been engaged in a violently passionate and incestuous affair with her brother but was simultaneously involved in an adulterous relationship with Coleridge, becoming pregnant twice and contriving abortions by means of powerful drugs.

But that is the subject of another book.

By the age of twenty, Tom's linguistic genius was acknowledged by the Bishopric of York which invited him to work on a new translation of the Bible. Shortly afterwards he was falsely arraigned on a charge of rape by a magistrate's wife — in those days a capital offence — but for some reason, hidden from him until he was over forty, the charge was dropped. Tom undoubtedly attributed his good fortune to the dagger whereupon he forsook his religious beliefs, becoming an agnostic.

Subsequently he served under the Duke of Wellington in Spain throughout the entire Peninsular War, and though he and his famous horse, Blackie, took part in over a hundred cavalry charges, he never sustained the slightest wound, both Tom and the dagger becoming legends.

His immunity to death and injury continued until the Battle of Waterloo when a French musket ball hit him squarely in the middle, only to be deflected by the Silver Dagger which was blasted from his belt. No sooner had this happened than he was cut off by eight French *Cuirassiers*, more than a match for even a man of his tremendous power.

Faced with certain death — and no longer protected by the Silver Dagger — he described seeing a vision, that of his lost love for whom he had kept a cruel pledge of silence for over twenty years. Without knowing why, he began to recite part of the 91st Psalm in French 'in a voice which was not my own'.

On hearing an Englishman quoting from the Bible in their own tongue his adversaries held back, seemingly afraid of what they had heard. Before they were able to renew their attack, a stray Congreve rocket fell behind them, entirely off course as were most of these unpredictable projectiles, the hissing horror killing four of them instantly. In the turmoil, Tom beheaded two others and effected his escape.

As a result of this episode Tom came to believe that the Silver Dagger was, in reality, an instrument of God in whom he resumed his belief.

The French artillery had been inflicting terrible carnage upon the infantry and the smoke from the cannonade made it impossible to see more than five yards. Hearing a trumpeter (Reeves) sound a 'Rally', Tom moved in the direction of the call. There, where the air was clearer, he saw cavalrymen swarming in from all sides. He took command of what Blues and Royals were present, leading them up an *arrête* and fell upon the French artillery from the right flank.

There they sabred the gunners, slashed the horses' throats, slew the drivers and put seventy-four guns out of action in the space of ten minutes before descending from the ridge and returning to their lines. The Marquis of Anglesea regarded this as a turning point in the battle for it took the enemy an hour to bring the guns into action again. What the outcome of the conflict would have been if the dagger had not saved Tom's life can be no more than conjecture. Or what the effect would have been upon civilization if the power-crazed Napoleon had been the victor and vented his acid spleen upon the vanquished. But this was not to be: the Silver Dagger had exercised its power and influence over Europe for the next hundred years.

Following this, Tom married the daughter of his first love and achieved the happiness which had previously eluded him, sharing an idyllic marriage which lasted for almost sixty years.

And the Silver Dagger of Owain Gwynedd? Perhaps it still lies buried on the field of Waterloo. If it had been recovered there can be little doubt that the world would have already felt its influence. Unless, of course, it is still waiting to be found by its next rightful owner. . .

THE BARD'S TALES

THE LAKE OF THE FAIR ONES

Ancient legends of the Fairies one of whose descendants was still alive in 1938

Lyn Cwellyn nestles comfortably between the western flank of Snowdon and the eastern lee of Mynydd Mawr (The Big Mountain), some four miles north of Beddgelert. And while it has no pretensions to great beauty, it possesses a magic all of its own. Once this placid lake was referred to as *Tarddeni* (The Outpouring), though whether this alluded to the waters themselves or the anecdotal zeal of the locals is a matter of some conjecture.

In the late thirties I had the good fortune to attend an Y Tair Ysbrydnos (Ghost Night) held at Beddgelert on the Eve of St John. In keeping with the usual practice during Story Telling Evenings, I anticipated that the entertainment would be monopolized by the *taids* (grandfathers). As things turned out, this was an exception for, on the stroke of eight, a lady rose from her seat.

She was of diminutive proportions with flaxen hair cascading to her slender waist, and though she possessed the most mischievous and bluest eyes imaginable and a flawless, fair complexion, she diffused an aura of rare maturity. During a typically warm, Welsh welcome — an oration which proclaimed that the speaker had received an unusually fine education — I attempted to assess her age but this proved to be an insoluble enigma.

'I am Olwyn Davies, housewife, mother and student of Welsh history', her melodious voice intoned. 'Tonight we are graced by the presence of many English guests. Consequently, rather than devote the entire evening to Ghost-Stories, many of which, I fear, are the quixotic inventions of latter-day charlatans, we felt that the first half of the *divertissement* should be given to tales of greater substance, that is to say, the *Tylwyth Teg*. The literal translation of this is The Fair Ones but it really means The Fairies.

'Those who live to the east of Offa's Dyke are probably sceptical regarding the existence of hyperphysical beings. But, dear friends, you are in Gwynedd and perhaps when we have each recounted our Tales, you may join your children and once again believe in Fairy Stories.'

Her lilting speech was captivating and her smile, one of mesmeric enchantment. Pressure of space renders it impossible to record the whole of her almost poetic narration but the substance was as follows:-

'I am not a native of Nant Betws, having been brought here as a bride of nineteen some sixty years ago. . .'

The effect was electric. It was inconceivable that a woman of her beauty and vivacity could be almost eighty. The interest of the non-Gwyneddan element was instantly galvanized. She continued, obviously aware that the audience was eating out of the palm of her hand.

'Legend has it that the Fair Ones are descended from the souls of virtuous Druids. The advent of Christianity, however, rendered it necessary to repudiate this belief, whereupon an equally unbelievable myth took root in Anglesea that their real genesis lay in the Holy Land. The story put out is somewhat reminiscent of the Old Woman who lived in a shoe and had so many children she didn't know what to do. Their version was that when Christ approached the home of a woman who had borne over twenty children, she became fearful that He would chastize her for undue profligacy. Accordingly, she hid half of her brood in a nearby cave and these children, believing that their mother's refusal to let them touch Jesus must mean that they were accursed, disappeared into the uttermost depths of the cavern and on finally reaching the Other World became the progenitors of The Fairies.

'Nothing could be further from the truth for though their realm is certainly located beneath the earth's surface, they are indigenous to Wales being ruled by King Gwyn ap Nudd who, from time immemorial, has dwelt in the vicinity of the Berwyns. Indeed, the very name *Berwyn* is the metathetical reconstruction of Bre Wyn, that is, The Hill of Gwyn. So, you may wonder, who are these denizens of the Other World.'

She went on to explain that access to the Other World was by way of caves, holes in the earth, lakes and the sea itself. Evidence of this had been given by a number of people who, having actually visited this subterranean habitat, were able to describe it in full. Thus, the domain of the Fair Ones was known to be a haven of peace and plenty in which happiness reigned supreme, its inhabitants sleeping on golden beds adorned with coverlets of the finest silk, and where wond'rous music constantly filled one's ears.

She informed us that Fairies varied in size from that of humans to those who ride white horses no bigger than a hare; while there were some so tiny that they could dance atop the rushes, hide within fox-gloves and play beneath the heather.

The smaller species were of a gently impish nature, rewarding honesty with benevolence; but the tallest ones, though of a convivial and sociable temperament, were not averse to stealing butter and cheese, and would sometimes even milk a cow. All of them detested lies and uncleanness, and would readily put a curse upon any who ploughed through their dancing rings.

During the day, they all remained hidden, emerging only in the evenings when they danced in the moonlight, often circling round glow-worms, and sang in the sweetest voices to an accompaniment of harps until cock-crow when they instantly returned to their own kingdom.

'There is little doubt', she concluded, 'that the *Tylwyth Teg* made Llyn Cwellyn their own special lake and it is what occurs upon its shores between dusk and dawn which is of the greatest interest as my colleagues will now recall.' A white-beard struggled to his feet. 'Our immortal compatriots have forever possessed the wisdom of the ages', he started off, 'especially with regard to curing ailments. Doctors dismiss these remedies as quackery but my story will prove otherwise.'

IVOR'S STORY. 'The Fair Ones have always known that fox-glove tea relieves heart troubles, and untreated moleskins worn upon the chest ward off asthma. They knew, too, that speedwell heals impetigo and cures haemorrhoids; that putting one's stocking or sock on the left foot first is a great psychological palliative for rheumatism, while unpeeled potatoes carried in both coat pockets will almost certainly ensure a measure of relief from that condition particularly if they are switched about regularly, as will wearing a copper band on the left wrist. They also discovered the best dysentery cure ever known, better by far than anything old Doctor Powell used to hand out. You cut nine strips of bramble and boil them in milk with other herbs and if you drink half a cup of this potion three times a day, you'll be cured in no time. And while modern upstarts laugh at these remedies, I have never met anyone yet who has tried them and not felt better.

'Many present tonight will vouch that my grandfather started to go bald at forty. His mother-in-law, who knew more about the Fairies than most, told him to rub the fingernails of one hand against those of the other for at least ten minutes each day and, as God is my judge, when we buried him at eighty-two he had more hair on his head than Samson before Delilah got to work on him with her scissors.

'And I can tell you something else. At eighty, I became afflicted with the curse of old age — enuretic incontinence. Nothing the doctors gave me was a scrap of good. Then, one day, an old woman who lived by Bron-y-fedw and was descended from the Belisiaids advised me to eat a roast mouse every full moon and I swear on the memory of St David that I've never had a minute's trouble since. And I'm ninety-two now, you know.'

THOMAS'S TALE. 'Long, long ago, a tanner and his wife lived by the shores of Llyn Cwellyn. Despite being married for many years they remained childless. Then, one day, she bore a beautiful baby girl and their cup of happiness overflowed. Not long afterwards the moor people kidnapped their daughter leaving in its stead a weakly male child. Though distraught, the woman cherished the tiny changeling but it seemed to be wasting away.

'When the Fair Ones heard of this they told her that if she carried out their instructions faithfully the babe would grow into a fine, healthy man. Willing to try anything once, she bathed the little one in warm fox-glove wine, following which she sprinkled a handful of salt upon a burnished iron spade and then, after making the sign of the cross above it three times and flinging open all the windows, held it above a hot peat fire until the salt baked so hard onto the surface of the metal that nothing would stick to it. The treatment was so effective that the boy reached full manhood in only nine years whereupon he set out to find his true identity.

'Nine years elapsed before, at the *Calan Haf* (May Day), he returned with a beautiful bride whom his foster-mother instantly recognized as her long lost daughter.'

GLYN'S TALE. 'If mortals enter a Fairy Ring they can stay trapped there for a year and a day, the branch of a Rowan tree alone being capable of releasing them from their enchanted state and no matter how long they have spent there, they swear that it was for but a few moments.

'One day a young man fron Nant y Betws, who'd heard this story but considered it to be no more than an old wives' tale, passed Llyn Cwellyn where he saw a ring of Fairies dancing by moonlight. Brashly he stepped into the circle to join them only to find that what appeared to be no more than a mossy circle was, in fact, another world of infinite beauty.

'Some time later when the euphoria waned, he remembered that he had been on his way to visit his fiancée. On hearing this, the Fairies broke their ring and let him depart. Fearful that his beloved would be vexed with him, he hastened home to find both his parents had died, while his brothers, who hadn't seen him for seven years, failed to recognize him. Worse still, his loved one, believing that he had deserted her for another, was happily wed and the mother of two fine children.

'He returned to where he had met the Fairies but found no trace of them. Torn between this and the Other World, he died a week later of a broken heart.'

MEREDITH'S TALE. 'One night, by Llyn Cwellyn, a young man caught a Fairy and because she was the most desirable girl he had ever seen, he proposed to her. At first she demurred, warning him that although the *Telwyth Teg* could safely handle iron cooking utensils, they must never come into contact with iron knives or agricultural implements made from that metal. Undeterred, he took her to wife and she bore him a son and a daughter. One day a horse bolted and in attempting to catch it she was struck by an iron stirrup. She instantly vanished but soon afterwards her husband heard her voice coming from the lake:

> That our son may not be cold
> O'er him place thy thickest smock;
> Lest the swan-white one be cold,
> Cover her with her mother's frock.

'A very similar marriage took place between a Fairy and a man from Cwm Pennant. After bearing her husband four children she, too, was struck by iron and disappeared. But he was luckier than most because she met him regularly on an island which floats on Llyn Dywarchen. And, if you ever go to Eifonydd they will tell you that the fair-haired people who live in Cwn Pennant are known as the *Belisiaid* because they are descended from this Fair One whose name was Bela.'

The elfin figure of Olwyn Davies rose again. 'Finally I will recount a story from my own village of Bethesda,' she said. 'No doubt many of you consider the fear of iron to be an ancient superstition. But are we any better? Even today there is a legacy from the past with people believing that gifts of knives or scissors inevitably cut friendship.

'Llyn Corwrion, to give it its historic name, is a pleasant spot where, many years ago, a farmer was scything hay while his cattle grazed by the water's edge. His reverie was interrupted by strange noises. He climbed a hillock beyond which he espied a group of Fair Ones emptying cartloads of stone into a bog. In between times they danced lightly and sang in a hauntingly sweet fashion. And since they were the most beautiful Fairies in the world, with long flaxen hair and dancing blue eyes, he knew that they were from the caves near Cwm y Stradllyn just south of Llyn Cwellyn.

'He was quickly joined by his neighbour who was the rich and handsome heir to an adjacent farm. The young man could not take his eyes off one of the Fairies and, throwing caution to the winds, straightway begged her hand in marriage. Obviously she must also have fallen in love with him for she instantly accepted his proposal subject to two provisos — that he might never seek to learn her Fairy name and, even if she was very disobedient, though he may punish her with a wooden rod, she must never be struck by anything made of iron. Over the years they found the greatest happiness together and despite bearing many children during the next twenty years, she still looked not a day older than the day she was wed.

'There were varying reports as to how she came to be struck by iron but struck she was and vanished into the lake. Every evening for a year and a day her husband stood by the shore calling her by name but all he ever heard was fairy voices sobbing: "Belené".

'Years later, Belené's grandson fell in love with a beautiful maiden whose parents were so poor that they could not even offer a single cow as dowry. All his relatives, even unto the fourth degree, advised against the marriage, with his parents threatening to disinherit him if he went against their wishes. Notwithstanding this, such was his love for the maiden that he wed her and in so doing forfeited the right to be granted stock for his small holding of land. But on the following morning six jet-black cows and a pure white bull were found in his field and, as they multiplied, he waxed richer than his own father. Realizing that the cattle were a gift from his fairy grandmother, he named his firstborn daughter after her and thus a tradition was established that the eldest girl of each generation was likewise christened Belené.

'Thereafter the family fortunes flourished until the ninth generation when the line was reduced to one — a dashing young man of eighteen summers named Hugh who died unwed a year later. As he breathed his last, a plaintive cry echoed through the vale at which his vast herd of cattle walked into the lake and disappeared forever.

'Strange as this tale may sound, I assure you that it is true', she added with forceful finality. Then: 'If there are any questions. . .'

A distinguished looking man in a pin-stripe suit spoke out: 'Madame! I am a barrister and thus primarily concerned with proven evidence. You have assured us that the story of Belené is a true one. Are all the others equally true?'

'Indeed they are, sir!'

'In the legal profession,' he went on, 'we have a maxim which goes *falsus in uno, falsus omnibus*, that is, false in one, false in everything. Pray tell me, have you any evidence to substantiate one tiny part of any of these stories, or are they based solely upon belief and hearsay?'

'Are you a good Christian?' Olwyn probed.

'I hope that I am.'

'Have you seen God?'

'No!'

'Then your faith is also based upon belief and the witness of others, which is again hearsay, is it not?'

He smiled, appreciative of her rhetoric. 'No, madame! It is rooted in deeper conviction. To paraphrase the Bible, consider the sycamores of the forest, they reason not, neither can they control their destinies. Yet their seeds have wings upon which the wind carries them far and wide thus preventing an over-abundance from propagating beneath the branches of their progenitor where they would extract such a volume of water from the earth that this would not only cause their own demise but eventually result in the self-destruction of the mother tree, an act which, despite your assertion that Hugh's cattle put an end to their own lives, is unnatural and against the laws of the God I worship who, as the Supreme Architect of the Universe, granted those wings to ensure the preservation of His own handiwork.'

'I will not take issue with your proposition,' she replied. 'On the other hand, if I am able to prove *veritas in uno* and you are unable to disprove one iota, would not many construe this as *veritas omnibus*?'

'A judge would not but I would not be surprised if a jury did,' the lawyer admitted. 'And it is their verdict which counts.'

'Quite so!', Olwyn let fall. 'Now when Hugh died, as far as the law of the realm was concerned, the true lineage certainly ended for a bar sinister was not countenanced. However, seven months later, his sweetheart gave birth to his posthumous child and, in keeping with the custom established by her lover's family, named her Belené.

Thereafter, the tradition was maintained, and for what our antecedents would have described as 'at least thrice nine generations', the eldest girl was always so named. Neither did the traits change, all the girls being petite, with flaxen hair and eyes the colour of cornflowers. And time rested easily upon their shoulders.

'Sir! If I had not revealed my own span of years, without resorting to gallantry, what would have been your estimate of my age?'

'In truth, if I had said forty, that would indeed have been an unkindness to you.'

'Thank you,' she replied gracefully. 'Now Olwyn Davies is not my full married name. In addition, like my mother, grandmother and great-grandmother, and also my eldest daughter and eldest granddaughter, I have another which I consider my middle rather than my second Christian name for, good sir, it is . . . Belené. . .'

THE DYN HYSBYS
(A.D. 1240)

and

'Judgement Day'

(A.D. 1970)

Was this the 20th century outcome of his 13th century prophecy?

Since history was first recorded, man has regarded certain numbers as being invested with divine, magical, occult or sinister powers.

The Israelites were no exception, proclaiming that God, after creating heaven and earth in six days, rested on the seventh, which he sanctified. Subsequently the Old Testament became littered with 'sevens' and such was the Hebrew preoccupation with this number that, apart from certain exceptions such as Cain's sin being visited upon Lamach the adulterer after seven generations, it became synonymous with goodness, miracles and joy.

When, however, Jewish and Christian scribes narrated the worst depredations inflicted upon their respective peoples, they doubled their exalted figure to 'fourteen' and then contrived to incorporate this new and powerful factor into their writings, e.g. From King David unto the carrying away of the Jews into Babylon were fourteen generations; and from then unto Christ's crucifixion it was held that a further fourteen generations elapsed. Not surprisingly, fourteen assumed the mantle of doom.

Another number frequently encountered in the Bible is 'forty', though this is obviously synonymous with 'many'.

Gradually these numbers acquired such an aura of mystique that their usage still endures, i.e. The Running of the Bulls at Pamplona takes place on the seventh day of the seventh month; we glibly speak of seven-league boots; the seven deadly sins; the seven-year itch; and great happiness as being in the Seventh Heaven, while many believe that if it rains on Saint Swithun's Day, the wet weather will continue for forty days and nights. 'Fourteen', however, fell into virtual disuse, its omens too terrible to contemplate.

By the time Christianity reached the Atlantic, the numbers were revered everywhere. Everywhere, that is, except Wales! With

111

typical Welsh individuality the *cymry* turned for inspiration to the Hellenic Rites of Passage. Since these encompassed the three most dramatic events in life — Birth, Marriage and Death — the bards devised a unique triadic form of literary composition utilizing three as the basic mystical number.

The Mabinogion and early bardic poetry contain innumerable examples of triple acts, with the authors frequently employing the device of coincidence to intensify the fascination of their stories. But when the Celtic minstrels were recounting tales of epic proportions such as heroic battle-poetry, the uttering of curses, or the dispensation of charms to nullify spells, and where 'special effects' were called for, they did more than merely double their base number, they trebled it to produce the mystically powerful nine.

This ploy changed the face of Wales: the great bard, Taliesin, was said to have been born of the water of the ninth wave; in the *Mabinogion* romance, 'Culwch and Olwen', King Arthur's men slew nine gatemen who were at nine gates, and nine mastiffs without one squealing, while the giant Cei had these peculiarities — 'nine nights and nine days his breath lasted under water and nine nights and nine days would he be without sleep'.

When it came to charms, it was believed that eagles introduced shingles into Gwynedd[1] and that anyone who had eaten eagle meat acquired the power to cure this complaint and also pass on his 'magic' unto the ninth generation. The charmer, after spitting on the affected flesh and breathing upon it nine times, then recited the following poem to effect a rapid cure. (This translation is more in keeping with the spirit rather than being strictly literal.)

> Male eagle, female eagle,
> I send you over nine seas,
> Over nine mountains
> And over nine acres of barren land
> To where no hound shall bark
> And no cow ever low,
> Nor shall any eagle soar higher.

In time, the very social structure of Wales began to revolve around nine. A clan or sept had a heritage stretching back nine generations and extending sideways to the ninth degree. Thus, family ties were so immense and so jealously guarded that when the marriage of one of its members was contemplated, while relatives up to the fourth degree were normally consulted, the views of those extending even unto the ninth were sometimes sought.

The Biblical 'forty' meaning 'many' was too vague a span of time for the *cymry* who preferred the more precise calculation of thrice times nine — which safeguarded their genealogy and history.

In 1240, when all Wales was grieving over the death of their beloved Prince, Llewelyn the Great, one would have thought that the *cymry* would be in no mood to pursue petty disputes. But, being Welsh, they were! And because of that, what was little more than an inter-family squabble was elevated into a feud of such animosity that it threatened to disrupt the period of deep mourning.

Yet it was hardly a matter which could be brought before the Court of Elders which was far too concerned with the question of succession to consider lesser problems. Nor were either party desirous of involving the priests who inevitably considered altercations as being the wages of sin and were apt to do little but pontify, merely apportioning the blame and the financial penances involved, or occasionally referring the matter to the Bishop for the utterance of a curse rather than the resolution of the argument.

And despite the traditional Welsh love of litigation, neither family wished to call in the lawyers who were prone to utilize each case as a chance to advertise their own virtuosity in the interpretation of Hywel Da's Codified Laws, dragging out their briefs interminably with crippling costs to all concerned.

Fortunately, *Cymru* was blessed by an alternative and uniquely Welsh means of arbitration in the form of the Dyn Hysbys. These men had existed since the days of Merlin in the 5th century and although once regarded as wizards or conjurors, it soon became obvious that they possessed great ability, even their medical and veterinary skills surpassing those of the physicians and vets. Moreover, by the use of charms, they could cure persistent diseases and troubled minds, shield both humans and animals from all forms of sorcery, spells and witchcraft, and also nullify the most powerful curses. Equally importantly, their talent as arbitrators in family differences rivalled that of Solomon, while their faculty for being able to see into the future was demonstrated time and time again. These unique traits must have become hereditary for there are hundreds of recorded instances verifying their efficacy which still exists today in the wildest reaches of the Principality.

This Wondertale concerns a Dyn Hysbys named Maredudd[2] who was asked to resolve this quarrel which, in its complexity, would have confounded Plato himself — or, for that matter, any other philosopher who was not well versed in the legends, lore and mythology of Gwynedd. And could also foretell the future!

Maredudd acquainted himself with the substance of the complaint: that Emlyn ap Llywarch had abducted Margred uch[3] Meilor, whose father was intent upon vengeance. With Meilor being one of the Seneschal's deputies, and Llywarch a relatively poor man, there was no doubt that pride was at stake but the Dyn Hysbys divined far deeper reasons for Meilor's implacability. Maredudd's good friend, Iorwerth the Bard, had discovered that the Deputy Steward's intransigence regarding Llywarch's family was founded upon a sequence of numbers which had plagued their two septs since time immemorial. That being so, the situation could hardly have been worse. Accordingly he summoned both parties to meet him on the morrow.

There were nine present, segregated into groups of three. The first comprised Meilor, his wife and Margred. Directly opposite sat Llywarch, his wife — Ethil, and their lawyer — Tegwared. Separating the protagonists was Maredudd together with Iorwerth and Owen Bychan — the two bards conversant with the last nine generations of the respective families' genealogies. Emlyn was called before them.

Meilor presented his case. . .

The family, he vowed, had lived in Trefriw since the days of King Arthur, settling there after coming from Anglesea where his ancestors had dwelled for thrice nine generations. On the previous *Nos Calan Gaeaf*[4] the *Coelcerthi*[5] had been lit and everyone was enjoying the celebrations. At last, when the flames began to die down, the people started hastening towards their homesteads before they were caught by the dreaded *Hwhl Ddu Gwta*[6] and suffered the most terrible consequences.

As he and his family prepared to depart, they could find no trace of their daughter — Margred. Many believed that the Black Sow had taken her but Fluellen Bongham — The Hunchback — recalled that he had seen her and Emlyn hastening towards Llyn Crafnant.

At first, Meilor was not disposed to believe the lad for he was certain that his daughter would never consort with a Moorland man. Especially as everyone could tell from his appearance that the grandfather of Llywarch's great-great-grandmother married one of the *Tylwyth Teg*; and that Ethil was the daughter of Sian-coch whose very name and red hair proclaimed him to be a descendant of the Goidal Celts who, nine generations previously, had established a settlement of *Gwynddelod*[7] near Llyn Crafnant and were so primitive that they boiled their water by dropping hot stones into filthy earthenware cauldrons. That was the kind of people they were descended from!

Soon Fluellen's story was confirmed whereupon Meilor, his sons, nephews and male cousins collected their hounds and hastened after the young pair whom they apprehended on the summit of Clogwyn Mawr. There, Margred was freed and Emlyn taken to Trefriw.

'This is not the first time the *Tylwyth Teg*[8] or their descendants have abducted one of our children', Meilor stormed. 'Only nine generations have elapsed since they stole a perfect babe from one of my ancestors, leaving a weakling *plentyn newydd*[9] in its stead. For that reason we are still obliged to protect our children's cribs by tying Rowan branches and red ribbon to these cribs and surrounding them with iron as a protection against the yellow-skinned *bwgans*,[10] otherwise they'd still be stealing them every night!

'Now the custom in my family has always been that *Oed i gysgu*[11] cannot be agreed unless consent is given by all kinsmen to the fourth degree. Yet they once stole a chaste and marriageable maiden from my family,' Meilor recalled. 'I demand retribution of such severity that it will put a stop to these nefarious acts forever. And may the soul of Emlyn ap Llywarch be hunted by the *Cwn Wyler*[12] until eternity!'

'When was this other maiden abducted?' Maredudd asked.

'No more than thrice nine generations ago!' the other flung back.

'And with a generation being thrice nine years, that would be 729 years ago!'

'That is so!'

'I submit that this ancient abduction is irrelevant,' Tagwared interposed.

'I will take note of your submission,' Maredudd replied before requesting Emlyn to plead his case.

'Sire! Since I first cast eyes upon Margred my heart has been filled with a love for her which words cannot express, and from her glances I knew that she returned my affection. Even so, my heart was tortured by grief, for with her parents being Valley People and I am of the Moors, added to which I am descended by three generations from those who came from Ireland thrice nine generations ago, I knew that they would bear me the greatest hatred.

'Three months ago, Margred and I started meeting in secret and though there have been but three short trysts with none lasting longer than nine heartbeats, we know our love is greater than the hatred her family bears towards mine. Thus we decided to elope at the only time when we would have three hours start.'

Margred confirmed Emlyn's story.

'Dost thou love thy parents?' Maredudd asked her.

'Love them I did,' Margred answered, 'but since they now keep me from my beloved and seek to hurt him in revenge, I love them not.'

'Since you were in each other's arms for only thrice nine heartbeats, how canst thou be certain that you love him?'

'That I know not, sire. Love cannot be seen, smelled, felt or measured in time. Only those who have experienced love know the answer to your riddle.'

'Were you not afraid of the *Hwlh Ddu Gwta* on that fateful night?' he questioned.

'Nay! Emlyn assured me that the Black Sow could not hurt him neither could it injure me if I was in his company.'

Meilor rose, his face wreathed in a grimace of triumph. 'Hath not this stripling cast such a spell upon the all-powerful Black Sow that it cannot harm him, and yet another of equal potency rendering it unable to injure Margred while she is in his presence? Also, is it not true that during three assignations lasting no more than nine heartbeats each, he bewitched our daughter in so terrible a fashion that she is besotted with love for him and has forsworn that which she bore us? In having cast three such spells doth this not prove that he is a sorcerer who, being of the *Tylwyth Teg*, possesses the power to practice pagan arts and is thus unfit to wed a Christian maiden?'

'In the past,' Maredudd queried, 'have not the valley dwellers taken moorland women as wives, either willingly or otherwise?'

'Long ago that may have been true for they were privy to the mysteries of the weather and seasons; they were skilled in the irrigation of the land; they knew the secrets of the herbs and were gifted in tending the sick. Furthermore, they were valuable as negotiators in the barter of our tools, corn and cloth in exchange for cattle and sheep. In return, they lived a life of great comfort compared with their sisters on the moors. None ran away from us! However, our people have never sought Moorland men as husbands for our womenfolk!'

'But have not thy people raided the moorland homesteads to capture their womenfolk as slaves?', the Dyn Hysbys thrust back.

'Aye! But that was in the distant past.'

'Yea! Like thy memories, hatreds and prejudices — they are rooted in the sands of time,' Maredudd retorted. 'This is a case where only those who can see into the future may judge. Thus we shall adjourn to enable me to perceive what is to come. Return hither at noon on the ninth day henceforth.'

When the others had departed, Maredudd despatched Owen Bychan to Cororion where the Seneschal, Ednyfed Fychan, was staying, bidding him compose a ballad to elicit the truth.

It was obvious to Maredudd that the feud had nothing to do with young love. It was like a river with three sources: The Well of Ancestry, The Spring of Pagan Superstition, and The Fountain of Numbers. To Meilor, Emlyn's and Margred's happiness meant nothing compared with the perpetuation of traditional hatreds, prejudices and strife which dated back to five centuries before Christ.

On the other hand, Maredudd's prophecies were often no more than a professional ruse to palliate the lingering Druidical doctrines of immortality through rebirth and pre-ordination. That being so, rather than gaze at the stars, he knew he'd have to reach back in time to find an acceptable compromise.

The problem had really begun 3,000 years ago when the dark-haired Iberians settled in Wales bringing with them a hitherto unknown knowledge of agriculture and animal domestication. In time they became proficient in the use of bronze from which they fashioned weapons and farm implements. As the lowland forests were cut down to provide fuel to smelt the ore, arable land became plentiful enabling the valley farmers to prosper. And it was from these origins that Emlyn's family sprang.

Fifteen hundred years later the Celts arrived, tall as the Iberians were stocky, and with hair as golden as summer gorse. They came from eastern Europe where they had been in contact with the civilizations of Greece, Egypt and the Indus Valley. Consequently it was not surprising that they were a learned people. Their priests, the Druids, who were also their teachers, administrators and judges, established a school in Anglesea which became famous for its teachings of philosophy, history and poetry, the latter influenced by the epic battle poetry of Homer and Virgil.

And they possessed one great asset which ensured their dominance over the earlier settlers — they could produce and use iron, manufacturing shields and swords against which bronze weapons were of little avail. Their chariots, too, were infinitely more robust and they had invented a revolutionary iron ploughshare drawn by two oxen which could till land previously unusable.

It didn't take the warlike Celts long to dispossess the original inhabitants of their lush valley farmlands, driving them with their sheep, pigs and cattle to higher pasturage where the soil was poor and life infinitely more rigorous. Any who resisted them were slain or despatched to Anglesea where the Druids daubed their altars with their prisoners' blood before disembowelling them in the hope that their entrails would reveal the will of the Gods.

This was the people from whom Meilor was descended; arrogant, barbaric and quick to pick a quarrel. Yet, despite their military ascendency over those who became known as the Hill or Moor folk, the Celts regarded them with a superstitious awe, believing they were descended from the Fairies and had survived by their menfolk marrying immortal wives.

In turn, the Moor Folk were haunted by a dread of Celtic weaponry believing it to be endowed with magical properties and thus must never be touched. Moreover, the Druidical penchant for smearing their altars with blood had imbued them with a craven fear of anything red in colour, even the Rowan trees.

Whilst most Celtic children survived their births, an ignorance of herbal antidotes to puerperal fevers and infections led to many of their mothers dying in childbirth. The Moor women, being proficient in the use of medicinal remedies, generally came through their ordeal unscathed but the rigours of mountain life took an awesome toll on their infants.

In order to rectify this imbalance, the Celts carried off the Moor people's cattle and womenfolk, while their victims plundered the Celt's implements, corn and babies, sometimes leaving one of their own sickly changelings in return. As a result, the two peoples became alienated by an imperishable loathing for each other.

Therein lay the genesis of Meilor's bigoted opposition to Emlyn, and despite the passage of fifteen hundred years, the Celtic traits were still firmly embedded in his soul. A compromise appeared to be the only solution.

At dawn on the ninth day, Owen Bychan returned from Bangor bearing a report which enabled Maredudd to perceive how Meilor's Druidical beliefs, his fear of the supernatural, and his obsession with numbers could be turned against him.

The lovers' dilemma was something different. The future clearly showed that their immediate destinies lay elsewhere. On the other hand, they would certainly meet again. But a vague date wouldn't be good enough for them; he'd have to do better than that. In which case, with numbers having such a tremendous influence over everyone's lives, he'd manipulate them to prophecy a time so distant that, by then, even this furore would be forgotten.

In that way he could arbitrate to everybody's satisfaction. Two young hearts may be temporarily bruised but they would quickly mend, as they always did, when new loves came into their lives.

At noon, the nine participants and Emlyn reassembled.

'Fear not', Maredudd advised the young man. 'Thou art not entering the lion's den.'

He then addressed Meilor. 'Thy complaint is that Emlyn ap Llywarch abducted thy daughter for which act he should be severely punished.'

'That is so.'

'Thou hast also charged him with sorcery in bewitching thy daughter and likewise casting spells of such potency that they rendered the all-powerful Black Sow impotent to injure either him or Margred. If this be true and punishment decreed, may not Emlyn seek revenge and with amulet, philtre or scarab turn thy wife into an owl as Gwydian did with Blodeuedd?'

Meilor's eyes advertised his fear. 'Then I counsel that his life be forfeit,' he stammered.

'To achieve that end he must be brought before the Seneschal,' Maredudd countered, 'and how can I be certain that he would countenance such a charge?'

'Since I am Deputy Warden to the Seneschal, I assure thee that I could arrange for the accused's trial,' Meilor put in quickly.

'I think not,' was the soft reply. 'Owen Bychan. Pray relate the happenings of the last nine days.'

The bard rose and related how, when the Bishop of Bangor heard that many of his flock still believed in pagan superstitions such as the *Hwlh Ddu Gwta*, he announced a night of prayer, invoking God to show his displeasure with those who had not renounced their sinfulness.

'Thus assured,' the bard continued, 'I composed a ballad in commemoration of the Bishop's prayers, presenting this at a sacred story-telling before Ednyfed Fychan. At the end of my song the Seneschal condemned the superstitious, giving due notice that should he discover any of his officials holding pagan beliefs, they would be dismissed instantly from his service.'

'Didst thou bear witness against me?' Meilor gasped anxiously.

'That I did not but there's time enough to make amends if need be!' Owen let fall.

'Since thou art haunted by numbers,' Maredudd put in, 'why hast thou chosen nine rather than the Christian number seven?'

'Because, like three, nine is hallowed', Meilor replied.

'Oh, Meilor! Thou holdest high office in this land yet thou art as prone to accept fables, myths and the fabrications of lesser bards as the truth veritable without questioning their veracity as would a simple fowler or swineherd. Hallowed nine is not! In seeking a symbol which would enhance their own heathen teachings, the Druids cast their nets deeply in time, seizing upon the greatest mythology of all for their talisman, that of the Eleusinian Mysteries

which were concerned with the Festival of Greater Mysteries held
in Athens each autumn and lasted for nine days. That is where thy
nine came from! As God is my Judge, thou hast verily become
steeped in traditional hatreds, grudges and fears to the exclusion of
love regarding which thou knowest but little.

'Love blinds the eye, deafens the ear and destroys reason:
because of love, nations have battled in war and been annihilated.
Margred is but a maiden of the tenderest years who hath not
previously been confronted by this immortal and compelling force.
Had she experienced love in abundance from thee, perhaps she
would not have sought it so readily elsewhere.

'I take it, Meilor, that after what has been revealed, you have no
appetite for proceeding further with the complaint of abduction?'
Maredudd asked suddenly.

'That is so.'

'And thou art still willing to abide by my decision?'

'That I will.'

The Dyn Hysbys turned to Margred. 'You may believe that thy
father hath wronged both Emlyn and thyself most grievously. Yet,
by the strangest chance, he was not entirely remiss.

'Since we last met I have scanned the future wherein I perceived
that there is no happiness for thee and Emlyn in this life. Thus, I
prithee, seek not to oppose that which is preordained lest the
misery be unendurable. Notwithstanding this, I assure you that
thrice nine generations hence you shall both meet again upon
Clogwyn Mawr and again be called upon to endure the examina-
tion of nine others.

'But in those distant days, life will be halcyon. A descendant of
the wisest man in Gwynedd, Ednyfed Fychan, shall sit upon the
throne of England bringing peace to both nations. Likewise, enmity
between Celt and Iberian shall be long forgotten and friendship
prevail. Go in peace and God go with thee all.'

* * *

Today, young people would never submit themselves to arbitration
of this nature, nor accept such a compromise solution however
ingenious it may be, particularly if based upon a prophecy which
would not be fulfilled for over seven centuries. Or, for that matter,
any foretelling whatsoever!

But in 1240 they did and although Meilor's and Llywarch's
families never became friendly, at least the feud ended. Emlyn
turned his back upon the Principality, gaining office in the Court of

Henry III, while Margred entered into a happy union with a land-holder named Gwylym who was related to the wife of Goronwy, son of Ednyfed Fychan.

As for the age-old question, do foretellings ever come to fruition, who can tell? But about 730 years after Llewelyn's death, an unusual 'Short Story' appeared in a very reputable newspaper. In order to conceal the identity of the family concerned, many of the names were changed and the location given as the Isle of Skye. Now, with the passage of time, that privacy is unnecessary and the story can be retold in its true setting — that of Gwynedd.

After reading 'Judgement Day' I leave you to come to your own conclusions concerning some of these ancient prophecies.

JUDGEMENT DAY

It was like walking into the lion's den or, more correctly, entering the dock at the Old Bailey with the jury riveting their attention upon my every expression and thereby forming an intuitive impression which no amount of evidence could eradicate from their minds.

I hoped that my apprehension was not transmitting itself as guilt to those who held my fate in their hands and whose verdict could destroy my entire future.

Six months previously I would never have believed that courts of this nature existed — modern counterparts of the invidious Star Chamber, above the law of the realm and against whose judgement there was no appeal.

Once, life was good. With neither my wife nor myself having brothers or sisters and being childless ourselves, together with us both having lost our parents at comparatively early ages, we tended to live for each other, pursuing our hobbies of mountain climbing in summer and Olde Tyme dancing during the winters. Then, four years ago, Mollie picked up a virus in the Atlas Mountains and, six weeks later, I was alone.

My only friends were members of the Dancing Society and with all of them being paired off, I had no inclination to be the odd man out — not that dancing appealed to me any more. Neither was there any incentive to return to the mountains where the grandeur can only be fully appreciated when shared with another.

Instead, I went on coach tours for my holidays: it wasn't the same but there was company. Last year I booked on one to

Snowdonia. On the departure day I was late arriving at the coach station and forced to share a seat with an insular looking lady, a sex with which I had had little contact during the last few years. And the prospect of travelling for hours with one who, in keeping with her refined appearance, would only indulge in gratuitous conversation was a daunting one.

But she proved to be an easy conversationalist. I soon learned that her name was Margery, she lived a mere five miles from me, and she had been widowed seven years ago. It didn't take me long to sense that she'd recovered from her ordeal far better than I had and it was easy to see why.

Margery was part of a tightly knit family, three of the four others being happily married with young families, while Julia — a University lecturer — was involved in such a long-standing relationship with a professor that her in-laws jokingly referred to him as the 'out-law'. And all of them had ensured that she was never lonely.

Since Margery and I were the only 'singles' in the party, the hotel manager asked us if we would mind sharing a table. Neither of us did and we were thrown together again. After dinner there was a get-together dance and though Margery swore that she hadn't taken the floor in seven years, you'd never have known it. Especially when we continued to dance a Highland Reel long after the others were exhausted.

This was Margery's first visit to Wales. I knew the area well and, revitalized by her company, the prospect of half-day excursions to low-lying beauty spots began to pale. Once more, the mountains called.

I hinted this to Margery, adding that travelling alone was hardly the best way of seeing the real Gwynedd and obliquely asking if she was interested in accompanying me.

She accepted the invitation, so I hired a car. The first day I introduced her to the magic of Aberglaslyn, leading her to the top of Cwm Bychan where she gasped at the beauty of Llyn Dinas shimmering in the summer sunlight. Next we traversed the Roman Steps and circled the lovely Mawddach Precipice Walk, following these by an exhilarating little climb to Pen-yr-Helgi-Du where she gloried at the sight of Tryfan and the majestic Glyders.

Not that this was real mountaineering but every step was a delight, as were those we danced away each evening. By then, Margery indicated that she was ready for something more strenuous and in the next eight days we ascended Mynydd Mawr, Moel Hebog, Moel Siabod, Yr Aran, Cnicht, Glyder Fawr and Snowdon itself. I was astounded: there was a lot more to Margery than met the eye.

The Roman Steps

The last day arrived and I'd promised to get her, somehow, along the Crib Goch ridge but, during breakfast, all Snowdonia was blanketed by swirling mist and driving rain. As a consolation, I suggested Gwydir Castle which enthralled her. Then, as we finished lunch, the storm clouds departed leaving a smattering of their fleecy brethren amid an azure sky.

Clogwyn Mawr! I hadn't climbed that delightful little mountain since I was nineteen.

'Don't look back at Llyn Crafnant until we reach the precipice,' I told Margery. An hour later she turned and a cry of ecstasy escaped from her lips as she saw the lovely lake glistening in the vale below. 'I don't think I've ever seen anything so beautiful,' she managed to force out.

As we stood by the overhanging rock I impulsively slipped my arm round her waist, declaring that I wanted this to be more than just a holiday friendship. A moment later our lips met for the first time and the Big Precipice became Heaven.

We met regularly after that until, six months later, I proposed. She didn't accept . . . but then, she didn't decline either.

'Thank you, John,' she replied gently. 'Only before giving you an answer, I'd like you to meet the family. . .'

Her words droned on . . . intimating that if they approved of me she would willingly become my wife. But if they didn't . . . well, there were fourteen of them, including the children, and she would never do anything which might disturb the wonderful relationship which existed between all of them.

'A kind of vetting?' I enquired.

'Hardly,' she assured me. 'It's just that we've always consulted each other before taking the final plunge . . . and we managed to avoid one certain disaster. You see, John, our's is a rather special case, isn't it?'

It was, and reminiscent of the ancient Welsh tradition wherein entire families were asked to comment upon a proposed match.

On the following Sunday I was ushered into Margery's lounge which took on the semblance of a lion's den . . . or the dock at the Old Bailey on Judgement Day.

There were nine of them present including Margery. On my left was Terry — an athletic Adonis with a first-class brain — and his wife, Diane. She was twenty-three and her welcoming smile matched the warmth of her eyes.

Next to them was Tricia, almost a classical beauty and immaculately dressed. Beside her was her husband, Richard, impeccably attired, his shirt proclaiming its Turnbull and Asser origin.

Llyn Crafnant

He was a solicitor and, at first sight, not a man with whom one could easily forge a friendship.

Then came Philip, an accountant, and his wife, Marion, who Margery had found to be a pillar of strength.

Completing the circle was Julia and her 'good friend'. She was forty-one and while one could hardly call her beautiful, her face was reminiscent of Margery's, except that she wasn't half as feminine and may be a *femme formidable*.

Margery introduced me. Terry's greeting was hail and well met and Diane's smile and sly wink convinced me that I already had one vote in my pocket.

Tricia was polite but somewhat reticent, whereas Richard's response was one of professional cordiality which, to those accustomed to their ilk, smacked at aloofness. It was clear that neither were impressionable and if there was going to be serious opposition, this is where it would lay.

Strangely enough, Julia's welcome was wickedly wry.

As if planned, the conversation suddenly erupted and, as I was drawn into it, I became aware that it was a subtle form of cross-examination.

Philip's passion was literature and he astutely probed my erudition. Luckily, during the last three lonely winters I had devoured Marcel Proust's twelve volume novel: *Remembrance of Things Past* — surely the ultimate in literary achievement. That startled him and he went rather quiet.

Despite Terry being impressed that I had conquered the Matterhorn and Mont Blanc, the Bakers pressed on. With Richard being Tricia's spokesman for the Inquisition, it was natural for a lawyer to couch his skilful interrogation in legal terms, but having handled the firm's legislative problems for many years, I was able to match his jargon and he eased off with a knowing smile.

There was a hush during which Margery suggested that we had a cup of tea. Diane streaked into the kitchen closely followed by Tricia and Julia, leaving Margery and Marion to arrange the coffee tables.

A continuous murmuring in the kitchen indicated that the girls were engaged in an animated conference. Suddenly the air was rent by Diane's piercing cry: 'What?' followed by a call for Philip and Terry to carry the trays.

My heart missed a beat as Diane burst into the room 'Hey! Julia and Alan are getting married!'

The effect was electric bringing forth a stream of excited congratulations. Only Margery remained seated, her face wreathed in such a complacent smile that I gained the distinct impression that the announcement had been stage-managed to put everyone in a good mood.

Eventually the babel subsided and they all regained their seats except Terry. 'Tradition demands that the youngest proposes the toast,' he began.

'I'm pretty useless at speeches,' he went on, 'so I'll come straight to the point. Welcome to our family, John, and may you both be very happy.'

I looked up and saw a circle of warm smiles surrounding me and heard Richard's voice: 'You've got a good man there, Margery. Look after him!'

The words had hardly died away before Tricia was bestowing a kiss upon my cheek. 'God Bless you', she whispered.

My mind reeled. Those whom I had suspected most were really just as demonstrative as Diane.

Then Julia stood up. 'As the eldest and, I hope, without my judgement being tinged with the effects of my own happiness, I heartily second Terry's toast,' she replied simply. 'We've heard all about you, John, and now, having met you, we're glad to have you as one of the family. We all know that you'll love, cherish and look after mum for us!'

THE LEGEND OF BEDDGELERT

The 'manufactured' legend and how it resulted in
Beddgelert being the only village in Britain to have its
name changed by an advertising 'con-trick'.

The lineage of Welsh Princedoms was not primogenital, the Elders
elected the most illustrious son. However, in his advancing years,
Owain Gwynedd, Prince of North Wales, saw that his two eldest
sons, Hywell and Dafydd, had become bitter rivals for the inheritance of his throne. Accordingly, he proclaimed that they
would be his joint successors, a device not only intended to stifle
their individual ambitions but also designed to ensure that with
neither of them being the sole ruler, none of their descendants could
claim automatic right of succession, a matter which, he decreed,
should be resolved by the Court of Elders.

Despite this, when Owain died in 1170, Hywell and Dafydd immediately mobilized their respective factions with the result that
the principality was riven in twain by internecine strife as the two
sides struggled for supremacy. Furthermore, with both brothers
looking over their shoulders for anyone who could be construed as
future or alternative rulers, there were many who slept uneasily in
their beds.

One of those in danger was Owain's grandson, Llywelyn, the
orphaned son of Iorwerth Drwyndwn, whereupon his mother took
him to the comparative safety of Powys, the land of her birth. Had
it not been for her foresight the subsequent history of Wales and
England would have taken a decided turn for the worse; the village
of Beddgelert would never have achieved its present fame; and
modern Conwy would have been deprived of an immortal link
with the past.

When Llywelyn[1] reached manhood he returned to Gwynedd
and laid claim to his inheritance with such vigour and military skill
that he welded together not only the principality but the whole of
Wales, eventually marrying Princess Joan, the daughter of King
John of England by whose side he sat as an advisor and signatory
in the drawing up of the Magna Carta.

Today, in the main square of Conwy, there stands the statue of Llywelyn Fawr (The Great), Prince of Aberffraw, Lord of Snowdon, 'an eagle amongst men' and a legend in his own lifetime: a man of whom a Cistercian chronicler wrote: 'that great Achilles the Second [who] kept peace for men of religion, to the needy he gave food and raiment, he gave justice to all, and by meet bonds of law and love bound all men to him'.

Seemingly, men were not the only ones bound to him by love. Even after his marriage, Llywelyn's retinue invariably included one or more of what a contemporary annalist described as: 'his beautiful Welsh maidens of the moment', one of whom became the mother of Gruffydd, father of the second great Llywelyn — the first native Prince of Wales whose title was acknowledged by the English throne. Unfortunately, he was the last.

Llywelyn also had two other great loves — his horses and dogs. And perhaps this snippet of information was the embryo from which sprang a legend concerning the living legend himself.

Prince Llywelyn was an intrepid horseman who enjoyed nothing better than a long day's hunt irrespective of whether the quarry was wild boar, deer or the occasional wolf. To facilitate his pastime he acquired several hunting lodges, one of his favourites being a fine wood *hafod* on the banks of the Afon Glaslyn near Beddkelert, a hamlet often referred to by its older name of Llan y borth. There, not only was the terrain ideal for the chase but it afforded the Prince an opportunity to visit his old friend, the Augustinian prior of St Mary's Priory which served as a hospice for pilgrims on their long journey to Bardsey Isle.

One day, Llywelyn went hunting accompanied by his wife and several retainers, leaving his baby son and heir, Dafydd, in the care of a nursemaid and male servant who, presumably, were something more than mere acquaintances. The pair waited until the sounds of the hunting horns receded in the distance and then, heedless of their immense responsibility, hastened towards the solitude of the surrounding hills, leaving their charge alone in his crib.

All morning the huntsmen scoured the countryside, the pack being led by Llywelyn's beloved hound, Gelert, whom a 'bard' described as 'a lamb at home, a lion in the chase'. Eventually, the pack became unusually restive and, as it began to split up, the Prince noted that Gelert was missing. Knowing that his faithful friend would never quit the chase save for the direst of reasons, the idea seized his mind that with a dog's reasoning and instinct being beyond the ken of man, Gelert must have returned to the *hafod*.

He thus abandoned the chase, leading his party homewards at the gallop.

When they arrived there, Gelert greeted his master in his usual exuberant manner but whereas his coat was usually smooth and gleaming, it was ruffled and spattered with gore. The Princess, who was no lover of dogs, immediately feared the worst and ran into the house where she found the crib upside down, its torn and bloodstained coverlets strewn across the floor and the baby missing. Her screams brought Llywelyn to her side and thinking that Gelert must have killed their son in a fit of jealousy or madness, he drew his sword and slew him with a single blow.

At that precise moment a plaintive whimper was heard from beneath a pile of covers under which they found Dafydd safe and sound. As Princess Joan clasped the child to her breast, a follower lifted the crib to reveal the body of a gigantic wolf which Gelert had killed in defence of the baby prince.

Needless to say, Llywelyn was stricken by the most terrible feelings of guilt both for having suspected his noble friend and then repaying his debt in such a dastardly fashion. With this in mind, he ordered his retainers to bury Gelert nearby, setting commemorative stones upon the mound. And, in order that Gelert's brave deed should never be forgotten as long as mankind remained on earth, he decreed that his resting place should henceforth be known as Bedd Gelert.

There is little need to enquire whether this particular legend is fact or fiction for its origin is now well known. . .

During the late seventeen hundreds, early travellers described Aberglaslyn as a fearsome place, John Craddock declaring it to be the 'noblest specimen of the Finely Horrid the Eye can possibly behold . . . 'tis the last Approach to the mansion of Pluto through the regions of Despair'. With human nature being what it is, descriptions like these attracted others and The Royal Goat Hotel was built at Beddkelert to accommodate the increasing influx of visitors.

The first landlord of this hostelry was a certain David Pritchard who hailed from South Wales and was a student of folk-lore. In an attempt to boost trade he decided to exploit the prevalent romanticism and, assisted by the parish clerk, created a pseudo-medieval cairn and mound in close proximity to the church, planting trees around it. This accomplished, the plotters then perpetuated what can only be described as a brilliant con-trick in launching the Legend of Gelert. This tear-jerker was later embodied in a ballad (or *doggerel!*) being reproduced on thousands of postcards, teatowels and even pinafores.

Be that as may, the ploy was successful, more tourists flocking to The Goat than pilgrims ever stayed at St Mary's hospice, all weeping unashamedly at Gelert's grave. And the name of the village itself was changed from Beddkelert to Beddgelert.

Pritchard could hardly claim to have invented the story which, in various guises, has been part of European folk-lore since it first appeared in Hungary during the 8th century. And there is no reason to suppose that it was not based upon an actual tragedy.

POSTSCRIPT. For many years Room 29 at the Royal Goat Hotel was used to accommodate one of the servant girls. One night, shortly after Mr Pritchard's death, the girl claimed that she had been wakened by his ghost which instructed her to tell his wife that she must dig up the hearthstone of the bar fireplace. Mrs Pritchard was naturally annoyed that the apparition manifested itself in the girl's bedroom rather than her own. However, when the stone was prised out, a vast number of golden guineas were found underneath.

The last time I was there, the old bar-room had been turned into a gent's toilet.

THE BLACK BULL OF GWYNEDD

The incredible true story of how prophecies made in the
5th century came to pass and resulted in the Black Bull
of Gwynedd (Henry VII) coming to the throne of England
and founding the line from which The House of Windsor
originated.

The story of how the Red Dragon was adopted as the emblem of
Wales is mostly invention but like many ancient myths, its subsequent effect was incalculable, providing the *Cymru* with a Stan-
dard round which the compatriots rallied in times of dire adversity.

'The Black Bull of Gwynedd', however, is not only a true story
with every detail meticulously recorded by contemporary
historians and official documents but also a saga accurately
foretold by the bards centuries earlier. How these seers foretold the
future with such incredible accuracy is a mystery we may never
solve, but if an author wrote a novel based upon such a surfeit of
chance and coincidence intermingled with an endless profusion of
intrigue, passion, arranged marriages, murder, bigotry and un-
quenchable lust for ultimate power, no publisher would entertain
it.

But this was the era of the Tudors, the gloriana which set Britain
on its course to greatness and led to Elizabeth II ascending the
throne. And, as such, it is the greatest Welsh Wondertale of all.

THE RED DRAGON OF WALES

During the 5th century, Vortigan, the last native King of
Britain, was so severely pressed by the invading Picts and Scots
that he invited the Saxon leaders, Hengist and Horsa, to assist him,
promising large tracts of land as a reward. Though he kept his
bargain, the avaricious brothers coveted more and declared war on
their erstwhile ally.

Vortigan retired to Gwynedd where he decided to build a huge
caer at Dinas Emrys in Nant Gwynant, the proven
site of earlier fortifications. No sooner had he laid the

foundations than they crumbled and sank into the ground. After this occurred several times his wizard-advisers decreed that the only way of overcoming the problem was to find a youth whose father was not mortal, kill him and mix his blood with the mortar.

Emissaries scoured the land until, at Caernarfon, they heard a lad named Dinabutius taunting another called Merlin because he was fatherless. Merlin's mother, the daughter of a king, confessed to Vortigan that one night, when she was still a chaste maiden, a spirit in human disguise had lain with her, following which, nine months later, she had borne a son.

When told what his fate was to be, Merlin confounded the wizards with a display of wisdom far beyond their own, finally declaring that the subsidence was caused by there being a hollow beneath the encampment wherein lay two dormant dragons, one white and the other red.

Vortigan commanded his men to dig deeply whereupon Merlin was proved correct. The noise awakened the dragons which immediately became locked in mortal combat until the white one lay dead. This Merlin construed as a sign that, in due course, Wales would gain ascendency over the hated Anglo-Saxons.

Henceforth, red was adopted as the national colour of Wales and the Red Dragon became its emblem. In a surge of irrepressible nationalism the bards foretold that one day, amid a golden summer, a great Black Bull would set sail from a land afar to slay the Saxons with his great ashen spear. Then, with the Dragon of Wales having turned the tables on the Saxon boar, the Bull of Gwynedd, arrayed in a shining cloak of gold, would have the English crown placed upon his head.

That the metaphor was mixed beyond all normal literary acceptance was of no consequence: to the Welsh it only served to increase the poetic power of the bardic homily. Although no hint was given as to when this would happen, such detail was considered irrelevant: a couple of centuries or so were mere droplets in the ocean of time and unless there was a danger of the foretellings not being fulfilled within thrice nine generations, they were not unduly worried. They knew that from this message, even in times of tribulation, hope would spring eternally. They were, however, more specific concerning the 'saviour' himself. Since the bards owed their origins to the Druid poets who once held sway amid the groves of Anglesea, they declared that the second 'Arthur' would arise in that blessed isle.

During the so-called War of the Roses, with the Lancastrians owning huge estates in Wales, they utilized the Red Rose of Wales

as their distinguishing emblem in contrast to the White Rose-en-
Soleil of York, the two subsequently being grafted together by King
Henry VII as the Tudor Rose.

THE BLACK BULL OF GWYNEDD

During the early 13th century, Ednyfed Fychan was Seneschal
or Steward to Llewelyn the Great in which capacity he established
himself as the greatest administrator of his time. Following the death
of his first wife he married Gwenllion, the daughter of Lord
Rhys, Prince of South Wales, she bearing two sons, Tewdwr
and Goronwy who, in 1246, inherited their father's office and
lands.

In 1301, Goronwy's son, Tudur Hen, paid homage to the first
English Prince of Wales who, six years later, was crowned Edward
III. Goronwy's great-grandson, Tudur Fychan, became a favourite
at the English court, styling himself 'Sir' Tudur and challenging
anyone who disputed his claim to disprove it in joust but such was his
prowess with the lance that none picked up the gauntlet.

'Sir' Tudur married Margaret, a descedant of Llewelyn the Great,
by whom he sired four sons. Of these, Gwilym and Rhys became
Captains of Archers in King Richard II's army, serving in Ireland
where they espoused their cousin Owain Glyn Dwr's (Glendower's)
nationalistic ideals. The third son, Goronwy, became Constable of
Beaumaris Castle and, in 1382, achieved the distinction of dying a
natural death.

It was the last of the litter, Maredudd (Meredith), who became the
black sheep of the family. Bishop Young of Bangor, who seldom
employed anyone who was not, like himself, an ardent supporter of
Owain Glyn Dwr, arranged for Meredith to be appointed Escheator[1]
of Anglesea, and there is no doubt that the young man took part in
the revolt against Henry IV when Owain proclaimed himself Prince
of Wales at the turn of the century.

Like many others, when hopes of victory receded, Meredith
deserted 'the cause' and, being penniless, set out on a life of crime,
casting his eyes upon the Holy Well of Llanddwyn in Anglesea. The
shrine was dedicated to Saint Dwyn wen (White Goddess) —
the patroness of lovers. Tradition decreed that sweethearts who

travelled there to have their love blessed gave generously to the already huge bounty held by the shrine treasury.

Although the raid was financially successful, the authorities soon identified the culprit. By that time, he was also suspected of murder and this alone was reason for Meredith fleeing from Anglesea. The more serious crime of pillaging a sacred shrine resulted in him being outlawed and forced to exist as a hunted vagrant amid the inhospitable mountains of Snowdonia.

Whilst in hiding, his son was born at Penmynydd in Anglesea. It speaks volumes for Welsh kinship that even after Meredith deserted him, Owain Glyn Dwr became Godfather to the child whose full patronymic was Owen ap Meredith ap Tudur.

The Stage of Destiny was then set. Despite the boy's indigent and inauspicious start in life, his ancestry was illustrious. As the following genealogical table shows he was a direct descendent of Llewelyn the Great through the latter's daughter, Anghared. And while certain annalists have questioned the girl's maternal origin — probably on account of political or nationalistic motivation — there is no reason to suspect that her mother was not Llewelyn's wife, Joan, thus giving Owen a lineage stretching back to William the Conqueror.

As Owen approached manhood, the outlook was bleak. The peace which Llewelyn the Great achieved was nullified by his grandson's lack of diplomacy in dealing with the battle-hardened Edward I who invaded Wales. In 1282, Llewelyn the Last was killed and the revolt crushed.

In retribution, the Welsh were dispossessed of many rights, outrageously taxed, and left seething under a terrible yoke of oppression. Worse still, Edward's employment of the Marcher Lords as his deputies created a society of 'them' and 'us' among the Welsh, for while the peasants remained oppressed, the traditional landlord class was permitted to retain their estates in return for fief and fealty.

During the 1360's the peasants' lot was alleviated by the Black Death. With half a million dead, employers vied with each other to attract a totally insufficient labour force. As a resuslt, wages rose dramatically and hours of work decreased permitting the traditionally low-paid to assess their real worth. Simultaneously, the bards became active, proclaiming that the Black Bull of Gwynedd would soon appear and rule over England. The seeds of another rebellion were already sown.

In 1400, Owain Glyn Dwr's revolt led to the worst situation imaginable, tearing Wales asunder as one faction allied itself with

OWEN TUDOR

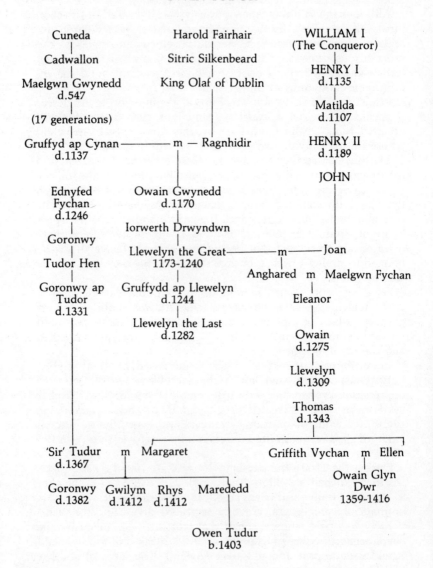

Capitals denote Kings of England.

what, as far as everybody was concerned, was a hated foreign power. King Henry IV already had enough trouble on his hands with Wycliffe's Lollards and other rebellions to devote all his resources to the 'Welsh problem' and while he was unable to achieve victory, he contained the uprising and imposed such savage laws upon the Welsh that they were reduced to serfdom. Thereafter they had no rights whatsoever in law; they were banned from holding Crown appointments; from marrying an Englishwoman; and their evidence was inadmissible against an Englishman even if charged with rape or murder.

By 1412 Wales was a scene of desolation. Everywhere buildings had been reduced to rubble or burned to charcoal stumps; monasteries and churches had been sacked; much of the land was left unploughed, and the flocks were decimated by plunder and neglect. In fact, anything which the English troops had not devastated, Owain Glyn Dwr considered as being owned by those sympathetic to the English crown and promptly destroyed himself. And by the end of the year, Owen Tudur's uncles, Gwilym and Rhys, had been taken prisoner by Henry and executed at Chester. A year later, Henry V succeeded to the English throne. Unlike his father, he was a capable general, quickly subduing the rump of the insurrection.

By 1417, Owen had grown into a tall and handsome young man with manners and an education to match his fine appearance. Being perfectly fluent in English and having a good command of French, he could have resigned himself to holding a minor but safe administrative post in Anglesea where an island 'civil service' had somehow survived as a buffer between crown and people.

Although the Penmynydd Tudurs were a respected family, Owen sensed an undercurrent of animosity towards him. First, he was related to Owain Glyn Dwr who had caused more strife than the English and left Wales in a worse plight than ever. Secondly, the ghost of his outlawed father invited many to whisper: 'Like father, like son?'. Others, recalling that his grandfather, 'Sir' Tudur, was a favourite at the English court, voiced a biblical condemnation: 'The sins of the father are visited unto the third generation!' Lastly, he was never allowed to forget that Gwilym ap Griffith, who had married into the family, forsook Glyn Dwr and changed sides when he smelled defeat. That made two turncoats in the family if you counted Meredith! So how could any of the family be trusted?

All this began to irk beyond endurance. Added to which, the traits of Owain Gwynedd and Llewelyn the Great were making themselves increasingly felt. To Owen, Anglesea was an open prison denying him adventure and advancement. Since these ambitions were unattainable in an English dominated Wales, he enlisted in the King's army as a hopeful stepping stone to a higher station in life or even glory.

His initial training complete, Owen was drafted to France where King Henry, with his army, was pressing through Normandy. Owen took an active part in the capture of Rouen and the advance upon Paris, whereupon the king appointed him to the Royal Bodyguard, raising him to the rank of Esquire. Subsequently, the king offered him a knighthood but the honour was beyond Owen's slender purse.

In May 1420, the Treaty of Troyes set out that Charles VI of France recognized Henry as heir to his throne instead of the Dauphin and, to cement the accord, gave him his eighteen-year-old daughter, Catherine de Valois, in marriage.

The union wasn't as cold-blooded as it sounds. For many years, Catherine's father had been plagued with recurrent mental illness, and with her mother being engaged in a protracted scandal with the Duke of Orleans, she had been raised in terrible privation, having once been taken a prisoner by the treacherous Burgundians.

Despite this, she possessed a lively charm and having inherited her father's good looks and her mother's beautiful eyes, she was known as 'Catherine la Belle'.

The outcome was that her respect for authority was scant and though she was strong willed, she had no desire for power herself. On the other hand, having been deprived of parental love, she longed for someone with whom she could share her natural affection. Marriage to Henry offered her everything she had never known: freedom from being kidnapped again and used as a political pawn; security from poverty; a life of merriment at the English court; and, perhaps, love itself.

Wisely, Henry insisted on meeting Catherine prior to signing the Treaty and it was noticeable that his instant approval was matched by her immediate reaction to his handsome features, athletic appearance and merry disposition. Almost at once they dismissed her chaperones and were soon seen: 'fondly embracing, the princess returning the King's kisses not in the least unwillingly.'

The union proved to be happy and intensely passionate but, ere long, Henry was forced to return to France where the Dauphin was contesting the Treaty.

On the 6th December 1421, Catherine gave birth to a son, Harry of Windsor, whom she took to France. The reunion was a sad one,

Henry having contracted dysentery from which he died on the 3rd August. Ten weeks later her father passed away leaving her infant son King Henry VI of England and King of France.

Catherine returned to England, a mother, widow and Dowager Queen at barely twenty. Parliament immediately voted her a generous share of her husband's earthly possessions; her brother-in-law, John, Duke of Bedford, was appointed the child's guardian; and the Royal Bodyguard — which still included Owen Tudur — passed into the establishment of the baby king.

Much as she had received, it was no substitute for love. She was a foreigner in an alien land, speaking little of its language, and having no influence in her son's education. Faced with a lonely exile — albeit preferable to life in war-torn France — she retired to a life of privacy.

As one would expect with a young woman who had inherited her parents' tireless and passionate traits, Catherine soon became bored and desirous of company which was not eternally female. During the summer of 1424, she saw several of the Royal Bodyguard bathing naked in the river near her boudoir. One of them caught her eye — a handsome, blond Adonis with laughing blue eyes. She learned that his name was Owen Tudor (now spelled in the English manner) and soon found that this proud Esquire's manners, gaiety and education matched his outward appearance. And, as a welcome bonus, he spoke French fluently.

Though by birth and stations they were oceans apart, in the weeks which followed they gradually discovered a sphere of their own where there were no artificial barriers to separate them. As exiles in a foreign land, they were both lonely. A soft enveloping tenderness grew between them nurtured by a conscious resentment that Fortune had cast them into matrices so cruelly unequal, while the despair of living in a world designed to keep them apart drew them ever closer together. Before long, Catherine's admiration increased to the state where she described Owen as: 'The Gentleman of Wales is a beautiful person possessing wonderful gifts of mind and body.'

Inevitably they fell in love and the dangers which should have been insurmountable were swept away as they committed themselves to each other totally.

She knew that when her son was taken away to learn the duties of kingship, the Royal Bodyguard would follow. In order to obviate the unbearable agony of separation from Owen, Catherine appointed him Clerk to her Wardrobe which permitted him to remain in her presence without arousing suspicion. Even so,

Catherine's entourage must have been faithful beyond belief for even when she and Owen wed in secret, the world remained oblivious of their liaison.

In 1431, Parliament made it an offence to marry the Queen Mother. A year later, by which time Catherine had borne Edmund and Jasper, Owen applied for and received Letters of Denizenship (virtually naturalization) in the name of Owen ap Meredith ap Tudur which excluded him from the laws against Welsh citizens.

Unfortunately, Catherine had an enemy — the Duke of Gloucester — whom she had inadvertently offended during a Court committee, but despite the birth of her third child, her secret remained inviolate. The Duke of Bedford, who was privy to her affair, as were a few others in the Court circle, counteracted any speculation of scandal until his death in 1435.

At last, Fate took a hand. In 1436, while Catherine was at Westminster, she went into premature labour, being delivered of a fourth child. Someone, no doubt for financial or personal gain, revealed the entire story to Gloucester who was then acting as the Protector of the Realm. He settled the old score immediately, incarcerating Catherine in Bermondsey Abbey and lodging her children with the Abbess of Barking.

Owen fled to Wales where he was fêted for showing the world that, despite Henry IV's edict that a Welshman was not fit to wed an Englishwoman, his own daughter-in-law had chosen one. (Well, they said, if he wasn't the legal husband, at least he had fathered her children — and they weren't going to quibble over small semantic differences in this particular instance!)

Like his father, Owen took refuge in Snowdonia but in contrast to Meredith's reception, a chain of 'safe houses' ensured his preservation.

Then, in 1437, Catherine died of a broken heart 'after a long and grievous illness'. Or so the official report said! In normal circumstances the curtain would have come down at the end of the play. But such is man's greed and lust for power that it was merely the end of the First Act.

The Council ordered Owen to appear before the fifteen-year-old king who naturally wanted to see what his 'step-father' was like. Eventually Owen was arrested on a trumped-up charge and thrown into Newgate prison. In November 1439 the king intervened, granting Owen a 'General Pardon for all offences prior to October' and conferring upon him a state pension of £40 per year.

When King Henry came of age he appointed Owen Constable of the Royal Parks in Denbighland and arranged for his 'uterine brothers' to receive a good education. Eventually the religiously devout but weak monarch knighted Edmund and Jasper and later created them the Earls of Richmond and Pembroke respectively.

Within three years the king displayed initial signs of mental instability and Richard, Duke of York, was named as Protector. This acerbated the old feud between the powerful Beaufort family — who were descended from John o' Gaunt, Duke of Lancaster — and the Yorkist faction, this culminating in the inconclusive Battle of St Albans in 1455.

Later that year, during a period of sanity, Henry connived with the Beauforts for Edmund to marry their daughter, Margaret, the great-great-granddaughter of King Edward III. Although not yet thirteen, she was an incredibly intelligent girl, already displaying the forceful nature of her ancestry. At a stroke, Henry secured the loyalty of the pro-Lancastrian elements in Gwynedd, Pembroke and Caermarthen, this undoubtedly being the most effective step the king ever took.

Edmund and his bride were despatched on a mission of pacification to Wales where their marriage had caught public imagination. The leading bard, Robin Ddu, prophesied that the new Countess of Richmond would bring forth a new 'Arthur' to save Wales. But, with the marriage less than a year old, Edmund died of a fever, whereupon Robin suffered the punishment meted out to bards who led others astray by false prophecy on matters of importance — he was promptly flung in jail.

Jasper took Margaret under his protection at Pembroke Castle where, in January 1457, she gave birth to a son thereby effecting Robin's release and restoring his reputation. Her brother-in-law suggested that the child be named Owen but Margaret showed her future political acumen by insisting that, out of regard for the English, he be christened Henry.

In 1460, following the Battle of Northampton, King Henry was thrown into prison, the Duke of York claiming the throne in his stead but, as a compromise, it was agreed that Henry should retain the monarchy for the duration of his life while York was created Prince of Wales and regarded as heir presumptive in lieu of Prince Edward. These terms heralded a violent campaigning season. The Lancastrians rampaged southwards. The Duke of York met them at Wakefield where he was soundly defeated and beheaded. York's son, Edward, took over the leadership, defeating the Lancastrians at Mortimer's Cross where Owen Tudur — by then over sixty years old but still bearing arms under Jasper's leadership — was captured and beheaded, his son escaping and taking refuge in the Welsh mountains.

The victor was proclaimed King Edward IV, Pembroke Castle surrendered and young Henry was lodged with Lord Herbert of Raglan, a kindly Yorkist who lived in South Wales, and with whom he stayed for nine years. Following another disaster at Tewton, it appeared that the Lancastrian cause was lost and it may well have been had not Jasper maintained a pugnacious guerilla war against his father's killers.

His efforts finally bore fruit. In 1464, Edward IV entered into a secret marriage contrary to Warwick's advice and interests. The Earl bided his time, covertly fermenting opposition until, in 1469, he went over to the Lancastrians. The king fled to the Low Countries and Henry was reinstated upon the throne. Jasper hastened to Wales, released his nephew and began mobilizing his fellow countrymen.

Six months later, Edward gathered an army, returned to England and defeated the Lancastrians at Barnet where Warwick was slain. A fortnight later, Henry's wife, Margaret, landed at Weymouth but Edward destroyed her hurriedly assembled force at Tewkesbury where the Prince of Wales and every male of the Beaufort line was killed. A few days later he put Henry VI to death.

By then, Jasper and his nephew were besieged in Pembroke Castle by Morgan Thomas on the express orders of the Duke of Gloucester who realized that, with young Henry Tudor being the sole surviving male with any pretentions to being of Lancastrian stock, if the castle fell the king would certainly administer the *coup de grâce* to his charge. Fortunately, David Thomas was not only a good friend of Jasper's but a better Welsh patriot than his brother. Within days he had smuggled Jasper and Henry through the lines of the investing force enabling them to reach Brittany where Duke Francis guaranteed their safety despite being offered huge bribes to hand them over to Gloucester.

In April 1483, Edward IV died leaving his two sons, King Edward V, age 13, and Richard, under the guardianship of their uncle, the Duke of Gloucester (Richard 'Crookback'), who immediately made the sensational — though spurious — 'discovery' that Edward's marriage to Elizabeth Woodville had been invalid under Papal law thus rendering the two boys illegitimate and therefore unfit to rule. He then claimed the throne, being crowned King Richard III.

The wearers of the White Rose relaxed. A strong Yorkist king reigned; his two illegitimate nephews were ensconced in the Tower — 'for their own safety' — it was said; Elizabeth Woodville was in sanctuary at Westminster which she dare not leave for fear of arrest; Margaret Beaufort, Duchess of Richmond, had acquired as her third husband, Thomas, Lord Stanley, who was a staunch ally; and, most importantly of all, the entire male Beaufort lineage had been wiped out. As far as they were concerned, the Red Rose had wilted beyond revival.

During the ensuing autumn, the Duke of Buckingham — whose powerful support had ensured Richard's succession — discovered that the king had murdered the two 'Princes in the Tower'. Utterly sickened, he decided that the present king must be replaced . . . by himself!

Notwithstanding her husband's political allegiance, Margaret Beaufort put blood before the bonds of matrimony. She contacted Elizabeth Woodville in secret and the two ladies hammered out a plan to put Henry Tudor on the throne with Edward IV's daughter, Elizabeth of York, as his queen, thereby ending the schism between Lancaster and York. She also met Buckingham privately, persuading him to abandon his own ambition and support her son. Following this she encouraged Jasper and Henry to gather an army and seize the throne but the king's Intelligence Service was up to its task so that when the invading force arrived in Poole, the element of surprise was lost and they were forced to return to Brittany. Buckingham was executed for treason but no one ever suspected Margaret of being implicated.

In desperation, Richard despatched an emissary to Duke Francis offering a 'King's ransom in exchange for the Pretender'. Unfortunately, the Duke was gravely ill and state matters were being dealt with by an unsavoury Treasurer named Landois who saw this as an opportunity to line his own pocket. Jasper was too old a hand at intrigue not to have his own spies in the right places and, learning of the plot, secured permission from the Regent of France for his party to be granted sanctuary, smuggling Henry out of the Duchy with only an hour to spare before Landois' men arrived on the scene.

In Gwynedd, the bards showed their impatience by repeating the prophecy and calling upon Henry to return at once since victory was foretold. Naturally, he didn't attend to their entreaties but there was another voice to which he was forced to listen. Henry had publicly proclaimed that upon his succession to the throne he would gladly take Elizabeth of York as his queen to bring accord to the warring parties. The now widowed Richard countered this by letting it be known that he was considering marrying Elizabeth himself — whether she liked it or not. Since that would wreck Henry's plans, he raised a massive loan and, early in August, landed at Milford Haven with 3,000 Norman mercenaries and 500 stout-hearted Englishmen. Many Welshmen joined him but, on reaching Bosworth, he found Richard waiting there with an army numbering twice his own 5,000.

Standing in the wings was Lord Stanley with a tremendous host. Henry requested his aid but it became clear that the noble lord's prime intention was to finish up on the winning side irrespective of which that may be.

The battle commenced with neither side giving quarter but the Yorkists suffered most, losing many of their leaders. Richard became impetuous and seeing Henry surrounded by his personal guard, led an attack upon his adversary with his Household troops. Such was the initial impetus that he achieved considerable success but with Henry's yeomen standing firm, the momentum flagged and Richard began to sustain heavy losses.

Stanley perceived that not only were the Yorkist irregulars inferior to the Norman professionals but, in contrast to the Welsh contingent, they were losing their appetite for battle. At this juncture, Stanley opted for Henry and entered the fray, killing Richard and making short work of his army.

The king's body was stripped of its finery and thrown on a packhorse, naked, as Thomas retrieved the Crown of England from where it lay and placed it upon Henry's head. The new king immediately showed outstanding ability in 'selling himself' to a country thoroughly tired of interminable war, and the populace joined in making his coronation a glittering occasion.

When Parliament confirmed him as 'King Henry VII — the lawful Monarch, Blessed of God' — Henry did not forget those who had sustained him. Uncle Jasper was created Duke of Bedford and his mother granted solus possession of her properties and estates making her the richest and most powerful lady in the land.

On the 16th January 1486, Henry and Elizabeth of York entered into a marriage of convenience to save the country from further turmoil and bloodshed. Their 'sacrifice' was at once rewarded for, almost miraculously, they quickly discovered a deep love for each other wherein Henry found that his bride was more than just beautiful; she was 'noble, gentle, wise and a loving wife and mother'. On the 20th September, Elizabeth presented her husband with a son and he discharged an important part of the bards' prophecy by shrewdly naming him Arthur.

Once more the bardic songs echoed throughout Gwynedd, only this time in honour of the Bull of Gwynedd who had fulfilled his destiny by slaying the Saxon boar and wearing the English crown upon his head. Whether or not Henry was arrayed in a shining golden cloak isn't known. But, by then, it didn't matter.

Author's note.

The Civil Servants in Henry Tudor's day were no different from those in office today. In 1549, an official records clerk dealing with Owen's affairs was confronted by his patronymic: Owen ap Meredith ap Tudur. Undoubtedly the poor fellow was ignorant of Welsh customs and assumed 'Tudur' to be a surname. Not content with that, he anglicized it to Tudor, losing Meredith completely.

Perhaps the error was fortuitous otherwise when his grandson came to the throne England would not have had a Tudor dynasty but one bearing a somewhat foreign sounding 'Meredith'.

Moreover, if Margaret Beaufort hadn't insisted that her son be named Henry, then Henry VIII would have been Henry VII because his father would have been crowned Owen I. Maybe Margaret had that in mind right from the start! Anyway, the following genealogical table shows just how Queen Elizabeth II is directly descended from Owen Tudor — the Black Bull of Gwynedd.

GENEALOGICAL TABLE SHOWING DESCENT
OF HOUSE OF WINDSOR FROM OWEN TUDOR

Capitals denote Kings and Queens of England only.

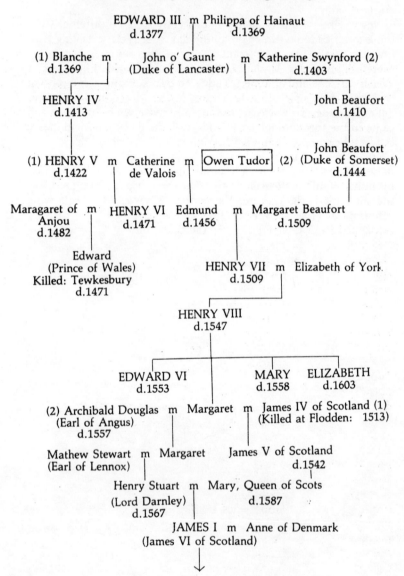

*From whom the Houses of Stuart & Windsor
are descended.*

GLOSSARY

The following short list of translations has been included for the benefit of those not conversant with the Welsh language in the hope that they will thereby be able to understand the meanings of certain place names and adjectives, thus adding interest to their journeys.

(arch) denotes archaic usage. Alternative meanings are given where these are in common usage.

Aber	River mouth
Adar(yn)	Birds(s)
Adwy	Pass
Afanc	Beaver. Monster (arch)
Afon	River
Annwfn	Hell
Annwn	Hell
Ap	Son of
Aran	High place
Arddu	Black crag
Artuir	Arthur (arch)
Arturius	Arthur (arch)
Bach	Small (masculine)
Badrig	Patrick
Banw	Sow
Bard; *bardd*	Poet
Bedd	Grave
Betws	Prayer house: oratory (arch)
Bod	Dwelling
Bont	Bridge
Bran	Crow
Brenhin	King
Bretwald	High King
Bron	Slope — of a hill
Bryn	Hill
Bwlch	Pass
Bychan	Small
Cadair	Chair, seat or throne
Caer	Fort or camp
Cant	A Hundred

147

Capel	Chapel
Cariad	Lover; mistress
Carn	Cairn
Carnedd(au)	Cairn(s)
Carreg	Stone
Castell	Castle
Cawr	Giant
Ceft	Ridge
Celyn	Holly
Ceunant	Ravine
Ci (cwn)	Dog(s)
Cleddau	Swords
Cloch	Bell
Clogwyn	Cliff; precipice
Clwyd	Gate
Cnicht	Knight
Coch	Red
Coed	Wood, plantation, trees
Coelcerth	Bonfire
Commote	12 maenolydd (arch)
Craig	Crag
Cregiau	Crags
Crib(au)	Narrow ridge(s)
Cribin	Crest of a hill
Croes	Cross
Cumraeg	Welsh tongue
Cut(iau)	Hut(s)
Cwm(ordd)	Valley(s)
Cwmwd	*Commote* (arch)
Cyfaredd	Charm or spell
Cyfarwydd	Teller of Stories
Cymru	Wales
Cymry	Welsh people: the compatriots
Cythraul	The devil
Dafydd	David
Din: dinas	Fort: city(arch)
Drum	Ridge
Drwg	Bad; evil
Drws	Pass; door
Du; ddu	Black
Dwr	Water
Dyffryn	Valley
Dylan	Tide

Dyn	Man
Dyn Hysbys	Wizard — but literally, a man of learning or knowledge
Eglwys	Church
Elidir	Riven
Erw	Acre: small holding (arch)
Eryr	Eagle
Eryri	Mountain fastness
Esgair	Ridge or spur
Fach	Small (feminine)
Fawr	Large; great
Fechan	Small. Junior (arch)
Felyn	Sallow faced; dark-skinned
Ffestiniog	Seclusion (literally)
Ffordd	Road
Ffynnon	Well; spring
Filiast	Greyhound bitch
Foel	Bare hill; round eminence
Fychan	Small
Gallt	Cliff; steep slope
Ganol	Middle
Garn	High point
Garreg	Crag
Glas	Green
Glyder	Sheltered vale
Glyders	Slippery ones
Glyn	Glen
Goch	Red
Gogof	Cave
Gors	Gold
Croes	Cross
Gwlad	Ruler (arch)
Gwyddfa	Wild place
Gwydir	*Bloody*
Gwyn	White
Gwynt	*Wind(s)*
Gwyrdd	Green
Hafod	Summer residence (High pasturage)
Hebog	Hawk
Helgi	Hound
Hen	Old
Hendre	Winter or low level abode
Hyll	Ugly

Ieuan	John (= Scottish Ian/Iain. Since Welsh, like Hebrew, has no 'j', Jones is a corruption of 'John')
Iwerddon	Ireland
Lefyn	Smooth
Llan	Enclosed area or church
Llech	Slate
Llechwedd	A slate slope
Lleu	Light
Lloer	Moon
Llwybr	Path
Llyn	Lake
Llys	Court or enclosure
Loegria	England
Mab	Son; youth
Maen	Stone
Maenol(ydd)	4 trefs (arch)
Main	Narrow
Mam	Mother
March	Border (arch)
Mawr	Great, big or extensive
Merch	Daughter; woman
Moel	Bare or rounded hill
Mor	Sea
Morfa	Coastal Marsh
Morwynian	Maidens
Mur	Wall
Mynach	Monk
Mynydd	Mountain
Nant	Brook; watered vale
Newydd	New
Norwig	Norwegian
Nos	Night; evening
Oed i gysgu	Marriage contract (arch)
Ogof	Cave
Olwen	Fair; beautiful
Pen	Summit; head
Pengwern	Shrewsbury
Penmaen	Rocky headland
Pennant	Head of a valley
Penrhyn	Promontory
Pentref	Hamlet

Perfedd	Central; middle
Pistyll	Waterfall
Plas	Large residence
Pont	Bridge
Porth	Port
Priodorion	Freeman (arch)
Pwll	Pool; pond
Pwyll	Intellect; common sense
Rhos	Moor; plain (or) rose
Rhyd	Ford
Saeth(au)	Arrow(s)
Sarn	Causeway
Tad	Father
Taid	Grandfather
Teg	Fair
Teulu	Household troops (arch)
Tewdwr	Tudor
Ton	Wave
Traeth	Shore esp. a sandy one
Tre: tref	Village (or) approx 16 acres (arch)
Trum	Ridge
Twll	Hole, cave or cavern
Ty	House
Tyddyn	Farmstead: approx 4 acres (arch)
Tylluan	Owl
Tylwyth Teg	The Fair Ones — Fairies
Uch	Daughter of (or) higher
Uchaf	Highest
Uchewyr	Notable personage
Waun	Moorland
Wen	White
Wledig	Ruler; prince
Wrâch	Witch
Y; Yr	The
Ych(en)	Ox(en)
Ynys	Island
Ysbryd	Spirit; ghost
Ysfa	Feeling; itching. (Also used to denote a 'sheep gait')
Ysgol	School or ladder
Ystrad	Valley or street
Ystwyth	Winding or bendable

A *very* simplified pronunciation of Welsh sounds — as much as a non-Welsh speaker can manage during a holiday! The penultimate syllable of a word is strongly stressed.

F   = V
FF = F
DD = TH
CH = K
LL = Th'l
E   = A '(i.e. Hen = Hayn)
A   = A (man)
I   = EE (Peel)
Y   = At beginning of word = U
Y   = At end of word = I (Rhyl)
W   = OO (Tool)
U   = Variable sound! Often as in 'Rug' but in Ddu, pronounced 'Thee'.

BIBLIOGRAPHY

The following books will undoubtedly be of interest to those who enjoy legends, folklore and mythology.

The Mabinogion, translated by Gwyn Jones & Thomas Jones (Dent)
The Arthurian Legend J. Rhys. (Oxford University Press)
Welsh Folklore and Folk Customs. T. Gwynn Jones. (Methuen)
Crafts, Customs & Legends of Wales. Mary Corbett Harris. (David & Charles)
Welshmen from the Earliest Times to Llewelyn. Stephen Thomas. (Western Mail, Cardiff)
The Ecclesiastical History of the English Nation. The Venerable Bede. (Dent — Everyman)
Historia Brittonum. Nennius.
De excidio et conquestu Britanniae Gildas.
White Book of Rhydderch (*Llyfr Gwyn Rhydderch*) National Library of Wales, Aberystwyth) *
Red Book of Hergest (*Llyfr Coch Hergest*) (1375–1425) Library of Jesus College, Oxford. *
Myth and Folktales in *Myth, A Symposium*. ed. T. A. Sebeok. (Indiana U.P.)
Celtic Myth and Arthurian Romance. R. S. Loomis. (New York)

* Translations, in folio, The Golden Cockerel Press, London. 1948.

NOTES

THE LEGEND OF THE TRIPLE SACRIFICE

1–3 Land was measured in the following way:—
ERW: The smallest holding = 1 acre.
4 ERW: 1 TYDDYN.
4 TYDDYN: 1 TREF (Family sized holding = 16 acres).
4 TREF: 1 MAENOL (Important family holding by fee payment.
Plural = Maenolydd).
12 MAENOLYDD: 1 COMMOTE (Often a gift by Kings to sons
and close kin. Holder often termed: Lord of Territories.
2 COMMOTES: — CANTREF (96 TREF. A Prince's inheritance).
4 Circa 1070 A.D.
5 *Hendre*: Low level homestead. During the summers, families often
moved to higher pastures where they lived in dwellings known as
Hafods.
6 & 7 *Caw & Peul*: Characters in *Culhwch and Olwen*, a romance contained in the *Mabinogion*.
8 *Môn*: Ancient name of Angelsea.
9 *Ynys Enlli*: Bardsey Island. Also known as the Island of the Eddies
since the tides which race through the sound can be a serious danger
to boats seeking the island's small harbour.
10 *Kelert*: A saint after which Beddkelert (Beddgelert) was named. Held
in memory by the Augustinian Priory there which served as a hospice
for pilgrims journeying to Bardsey Isle.

THE THREE SISTERS OF ARDUDWY

1 *Craig y Saeth*: Crag of the Arrow.

THE MAIDENS OF THE SEA MARSH

1 *Caer*: Castle, fortified dwelling or fort.
2 *Barfog*: The bearded one.
3 *Cadair yr Aur Frychin*: Llyn y Gader (Also marked on some maps as
Llyn y Gadair).
4 *Afanc*: Beaver or aquatic monster.
5 *Llyn Ffynnon Las*: Lake of the Blue Fountain — Glaslyn.
6 *Caer Fyrddin*: Caernarfon.

7 *Afon Dyfrdwy*: River Dee.
8 *Mynydd Bannawg*: The Grampians. Obviously an early reference to the Monster of Loch Ness.
9 *Mithos*: Myths (Greek).
10 *Annwyn*: The Celtic Hades.
11 *Mon*: Anglesea.
12 *Pengwern*: Shrewsbury.
13 *Wrâch*: Witch.
14 *Cymry*: The Welsh people.
15 *Cymru*: Wales.

RODERICK OF ANGLESEA

1 *Gwyn Felyn*: Gwyn of the Sallow Face — a noted bard.
2 While there is some historical confusion concerning her name, Mhaira vowed that it was Gwenllian.
3 *Uchewyr*: Notable personage.
4 *Ty*: house.
5 *Cariad*: Lover or mistress.
6 *Llys*: Court.
7 *Teulu*: Household troops.
8 Brook of the Beavers: Nant Ffrancon.
9 *Port Dyn Norwig*: Port Dinorwic — Port of the Norway Man.

MHAIRA AND MADOC

1 *Cynghanedd*: A uniquely Welsh alliterative device whereby consonants and vowels 'echo' each other.
2 An obvious reference to Newfoundland.
3 *Gwydians*: The Milky Way.
4 *Aranrhod*: Corona Borealis.
5 Hill of the Hawk: Moel Hebog.
6 *Blas Mynach*: A high point near Barmouth.

OWAIN GWYNEDD'S SILVER DAGGER

1 *Pen yr Ole Wen*: Peak of the White Light.

THE DYN HYSBYS

1 *Eryri*: shingles. *Eryr*: eagle.
2 Early spelling of 'Meredith'.

3   *Uch*: Daughter of.
4   *Nos Calan Gaeaf*: Night prior to Celtic New Year (1 November) when
    surplus cattle were slaughtered. Literally: 'The Night before the
    Winter (Calends)'.
5   *Coelcerthi*: Huge bonfires (Plural).
6   *Hwlh Ddu Gwta*: The Black Sow without a tail.
7   *Gwynddelod*. Irishmens huts. (Huts of the Goidals). Also referred to
    as *Cutiau'r Gwyddye*.
8   *Tylwyth Teg*. The Fairy People. Despite the literal translation being
    'The Fair Ones', there were two distinct varieties, one having yellow
    skins and dark hair, while the other was fair. Since the latter were
    sometimes referred to as being the souls of virtuous Druids who, being
    pagan, were precluded from entering Heaven, the distinction between
    the two types is possibly an allusion parallel to mortals of Iberian and
    Celtic origins. It was said that their height varied from 12 inches to
    that of mortal people.
9   *Plentyn newydd*: a changeling.
10 *Bwgan*: Goblin.
11 *Oed i gysgu*: Contract stipulating the appointed time for a couple to
    sleep together, i.e. marriage.
12 *Cwn Wyler*: Literally 'The Sky Dogs'. These Dogs of Death were sup-
    posed to hunt the souls of the accursed after their death.

THE LEGEND OF BEDDGELERT

1   In this story the alternative spelling of Llywelyn has been used, i.e. the
    one used today on Ordnance Survey maps.

THE BLACK BULL OF GWYNEDD

1   *Escheator*. Official responsible for the transfer of property to the Lord
    of the Manor or Cantref upon the owner dying inestate or without
    heir(s).